Sitting Pretty

The girlfriend's guide to a mindful (and joyful) life

Laurie Goldey, MFT

BALBOA.
PRESS

A DIVISION OF HAY HOUSE

Balboa Press books may be ordered through booksellers or by contacting:

Balboa Press
A Division of Hay House
1663 Liberty Drive
Bloomington, IN 47403
www.balboapress.com
1 (877) 407-4847

Because of the dynamic nature of the Internet, any web addresses or links contained in this book may have changed since publication and may no longer be valid. The views expressed in this work are solely those of the author and do not necessarily reflect the views of the publisher, and the publisher hereby disclaims any responsibility for them.

The author of this book does not dispense medical advice or prescribe the use of any technique as a form of treatment for physical, emotional, or medical problems without the advice of a physician, either directly or indirectly. The intent of the author is only to offer information of a general nature to help you in your quest for emotional and spiritual well-being. In the event you use any of the information in this book for yourself, which is your constitutional right, the author and the publisher assume no responsibility for your actions.

Any people depicted in stock imagery provided by Thinkstock are models, and such images are being used for illustrative purposes only. Certain stock imagery © Thinkstock.

Print information available on the last page.

ISBN: 978-1-5043-8591-6 (sc)
ISBN: 978-1-5043-8592-3 (e)

Library of Congress Control Number: 2017912437

Balboa Press rev. date: 08/22/2017

Contents

Foreword

It was a lovely spring day, and I was doing the laundry while chatting enthusiastically on the phone with my dear friend, Laurie Goldey. We were brain/heart storming about her incredible *Sitting Pretty* book idea. I was so struck with excitement for her because I could feel that this eureka moment was the crystallization of the skills she'd developed as a meditator, therapist, and poster child for the Western woman/girlfriend (think a deeply centered, uber bling-y Carrie Bradshaw, ommmming while buying her latest pair of Manolo Blahniks).

"You *have* to write this book! Women *so* need your message—whether they know it or not. Women like me."

The funny thing is, that during this very conversation, on this very spring day, I was multitasking (of course I was—that's the way I roll—or the way I used to roll, back in my pre-*Sitting Pretty* days). I stopped in my tracks when I realized I had just taken my freshly laundered sheets from the dryer and put them back into the washing machine. As my clean sheets, now slathered with detergent, were being doused with water, and my dirty laundry was still sitting—not pretty—in the hamper, I interrupted Laurie as she was effusing the virtues of how important it is that women learn to be present to the task at hand.

I confessed, "I was so wrapped up in our conversation that I just lost my mind and was *not* paying attention to the task at hand. In my attempt to multitask, I actually created more work for myself!"

We laughed hysterically at this very clear message from the universe. What if the modern-day message for women isn't (as Jack Kornfield's book is entitled), "after the ecstasy, the laundry"? What if the modern message for modern women, who want to truly find fulfillment in their lives, is more about bringing the light of awareness *to* the laundry—without skipping a beat. Or better yet, becoming so present while doing the laundry (and other seemingly mundane tasks) that we discover the source of true enlightenment?

What if it's possible to have a life where you're sitting pretty—no matter what's going on around you? What if you could be the light bulb you are, shining at full wattage even when tending to your screaming kids, grocery shopping for the umpteenth time this week, working late hours to shatter your career's glass ceiling, bringing home the veggie bacon, frying it up in a non-toxic, no-stick pan, working out in your hot-yoga/ piloxing/cardio-barre gym to keep your body as close to Forever 21 as possible, playing taxi driver to all the neighborhood kids in the carpool, redecorating your living room to cover up the dog vomit stain on the carpet, and, oh yes, making love to your "relationship-in-the-night" beloved spouse/partner? Whew!

"But, but, but," complains the hyperventilating modern woman, "there's not enough time to get all that I need to get done in a day and be present! Are you kidding me? That's a luxury I can't afford, not with my kids/boss/husband/dog!"

But what if it was?

One of the best things I've learned from Laurie Goldey's *Sitting Pretty* is when I pay attention to the task at hand, it's as if I'm given a hall pass from *The Matrix* and am able to *expand* time (as strange and hard to imagine as that may seem). When I'm sitting pretty, I mysteriously end up with more time to do the things I love—and the things I must do to keep my universe spinning—and I become meditation in motion, doing my life with gratitude, a peacefulness, and (dare I say) grace, rather than the bull-in-a-china-shop-way I roll when I'm hurling myself mindlessly through life, just trying to get it all done without getting arrested.

During the Vancouver Peace Summit in 2009, His Holiness, the Dalai Lama said, "The world will be saved by the Western woman."

I believe he was talking about you.

I also believe that this new frontier we modern women face is no longer about proving we can do/have/be anything we set our minds on.

Check. Already done that.

The next question we face on our new frontier is this: Can we live our lives with presence, awareness, peace, and mindfulness?

In other words, can we have our lives without our lives having us?

As we read *Sitting Pretty*, we learn that life is not a race, and it certainly is not about doing it all perfectly. We discover that simple tasks can become a meditation on being grateful for our coffee, for the water spouting effortlessly out of our shower, for the car we get to drive through traffic, for the traffic that must mean we're in a place lots of people want to be, for the clients we get to work with (once traffic dissipates), and for the clean sheets we get to come home to at the end of the night (that have been washed twice, thank you) to roll around in when we make love to our beloved.

The message of *Sitting Pretty* is a simple one: it's about taking a stand for yourself by sitting down (literally or metaphorically) in the midst of your busy day, taking deep breaths, and filling yourself with gratitude while noticing the abundant gifts you've been given. And in so doing, you develop habits and model this behavior for your children. The ripple effect is a more sane, present, peaceful world. That's all.

Ever since that fateful day when I washed my sheets twice, I've been telling my friends about *Sitting Pretty*. This is not only a book I need—it's a book I want to give to everyone I meet. For selfish reasons. I want to live in a world that is full of people who are filled with presence.

If you're a modern women like me (and I don't think you'd have picked this book up if you weren't), do yourself a favor and buy at least ten of these books to gift to your sisters, mothers, girlfriends, colleagues, or anyone who needs Prozac, therapy, gossip, or cocktails to get through the day. Or anyone who has ever washed her sheets twice by accident. Tell them that if they follow the suggestions in this deceptively simple book, they will discover an increased level of fulfillment and joy, not to mention an appreciation for their life exactly as it is. And as you do this, you'll be, in effect, joining Laurie and I in co-creating a world where all people can be sitting pretty, whether they are standing, walking, or even running. One task at a time. One breath at a time. And one moment of awe at a time.

Oh yes, tell them they're not allowed to read this book on the treadmill. You'll be watching.

—Kelly Sullivan Walden (aka Doctor Dream), best-selling author of *I Had the Strangest Dream, Dreaming Heaven, Chicken Soup for the Soul: Dreams & Premonitions, The Love, Sex & Relationship Dream Dictionary,* and *Dream Oracle Cards*

Introduction

Practice, practice, practice ... that's all I heard as a kid. If you want to be good at something, just apply yourself, repeat, and you'll excel.

But practicing didn't help me when I turned thirty. Maybe I was practicing the wrong things. That's when I hit rock bottom. Perhaps that's a bit dramatic—I wasn't an addict or desperate exactly, but I felt anxious, unsure and overextended 24/7. I was looking for something to *happen* to me so that I could finally experience contentment. But fulfillment wasn't happening. There I was, married seven years to a man I thought was my soul mate, but our relationship was falling apart. I was also miserable in my job as a marketing manager working in the (male-dominated) pharmaceutical industry, reporting to various people who seemed bent on taking credit for my work and making unreasonable demands. Besides all that, I was in major debt. For years, I'd fed my anxiety and my insatiable hunger for *something* with mindless shopping.

I needed to make a change, and a big one. So, after much deliberation, I ended my marriage (luckily, we didn't have kids together) and moved to Los Angeles from New Jersey. I was ashamed of my failure as a wife, but I was guardedly optimistic that a new coast could bring a new beginning. Basically, I ran three thousand miles away.

Yet my restlessness followed me to California, despite the perfect weather and the seemingly cool marketing job I scored at an indie record label, complete with a bungalow-style office in Malibu overlooking the ocean. What could be bad? Except once the novelty had worn off, I realized that my new job was as stressful and meaningless as my old one. Same unsettled, discontented life, different place.

Ultimately, a series of girlfriends saved me.

The first true friend I met, Lola, was an incredible coworker, a woman who exuded the bliss I was so desperately seeking. She was barely five foot tall, with exotic features, deep brown hair, and tawny skin. Whatever was going on, she always seemed to cope with a smile and an abundance of patience. We would do our jobs together, side by side, in our little bungalow where she'd hum like a little birdy from *Snow White and the Seven Dwarfs*. I was newly single in LA, adjusting to my new life; she was long married. On the surface, we didn't have much in common, but it struck me that she had learned to accept her life and had mastered the art of staying centered and being fully present. Whenever a supervisor would freak out, Lola would listen intently and calmly with a curious, open look. I was in awe of her disposition and her ability to let stress roll off her back. I had no idea how she did it. She practiced composure.

As we got to know each other, I discovered that her marriage had its ups and downs (like every marriage), but she was able to embrace it because she had forged a tremendous friendship with her husband. They respected one another. They had three beautiful kids, and she appreciated them too—despite occasional parenting challenges. And though she had a brutal two-hour commute—each way—she rarely complained. Instead, she seemed to take pride in her work, and she genuinely liked her colleagues. But what struck me most was her integrity. She was reliable as a friend and a coworker. She never canceled at the last minute like so many other people in my new town. She made sacrifices to put her family and relationships first by always being available to them, no matter what came up, because they mattered to her. She was discerning with her time, knew how to say no, and never complained when she had to go the extra mile for someone she loved. I admired that. It affirmed my own belief that relationships were what really mattered to me.

Still, I was surprised when she happened to mention a profound experience she'd had a few years back. "You know," she said, "I went to this women's weekend, and I think it saved my life. There's one coming up, and I think it could help you, too." *Saved your life?* "Hmmm, really?" I asked, trying not to let my skepticism show.

"Before that weekend, I wasn't a very happy person, and there always seemed to be a lot of drama in my life," she admitted.

Well, *that* made me curious. The forty-eight-hour retreat she described sounded suspiciously like one of those EST-like things, a throwback to the early 1970s. I imagined everyone crying, screaming, and moaning their way to enlightenment, which was not my usual go-to method for addressing my personal struggles. I preferred to hash out my issues with a good long cry, yes, but alone in my bathroom or on the phone with one of my East coast besties. Still, I was willing to give the retreat a shot if there was a chance it would lead me to a more satisfying, more meaningful, happier life.

Off I went, shuffling through registration lines alongside several hundred other women. All of us had the same look: uncertainty. I managed to hold off judgment, but I wondered if I was crazy to try something so woo-woo.

I wasn't crazy. Instead, I discovered that most of those uncertain-looking women were just like me: confused in their relationships, slightly dissatisfied in their jobs, craving connection and understanding. These were my kind of people—honest, vulnerable change-seekers. In one weekend, I heard stories of abuse, addiction, and neglect. The stories sometimes frightened me, but they also left me humbled. No matter what anyone said, the words were met by understanding and empathy from the group. My own story, while not as traumatic as some, was the truth. I revealed my struggles as a wife, a friend, and a coworker. I somehow felt understood by these women; they seemed to hold long and strong beliefs about themselves. I also learned about trust. All of us were in pain; all of us were choosing to reveal ourselves in that large auditorium off of Hollywood Boulevard so that we could move through our struggles. Together, it seemed, we might be able to face our challenges and shortcomings and lend each other support. I went home feeling encouraged, renewed, and motivated to take more responsibility for the choices I'd made, for the fact that I'd been expecting to lead a different life without looking too hard in the mirror.

I'm not saying that you can change your life in forty-eight hours, but after that weekend, I began going about my day-to-day life more deliberately. First, I broke up with a guy I hoped would be my future next husband. I realized that we were having fun, but if I wanted to eventually have a family, this guy wasn't going to cut it. I needed someone more serious, and I consciously set about finding him by asking friends to fix me up with anyone who might fit my desired criteria. That may sound unromantic and calculated, but I felt sure that true love didn't have to exclude certain factors that felt necessary to me, like security. Soon, I met the man who would become my husband on a blind date arranged by a coworker.

Just as important, I began searching for a way to make a more meaningful contribution to the world. I wanted a fulfilling career that would also give me the flexibility to raise a child someday. Eventually, with the emotional (and financial) support of my husband and parents, I enrolled in a graduate program at University of California, Northridge, and I earned a master's in psychology and education. The process took longer than I anticipated (school, getting pregnant, and accumulating the three thousand clinical hours required for me to get a license took ten years!), but when I finally landed my first job at a mental health center and a primary school, I realized how fortunate I was: I was working toward everything I ever wanted.

Almost.

On paper, it seemed as if I was thriving. Yet even after all the changes I'd made—new husband, new career, and, eventually, a beautiful son—on most days, I still felt anxious, as if something wasn't quite right. I'd checked everything off my list: great family, good health, dream career, cool car (this was California, after all), amazing friends, and meaningful volunteer work. It wasn't that I didn't appreciate my good fortune. Of course I did! I kept saying to myself: *I'm so lucky! What's my problem?*

My low-grade angst was ever present. Most mornings, I would wake up with a feeling of dis-ease or plain exhausted after a night of insomnia. I'd worry about trivial things, filling my calendar with lunch dates, vacation plans, and dinner parties to keep myself busy—anything to stop the chatter in my head. If I was busy, I figured it would be easier to ignore my stress and anxiety. Only the strategy didn't work.

Some of my girlfriends were feeling the same way. They would say, "I'm so stressed," "I think I'm going crazy" or "I'm running on empty!" I remember one time in particular when I'd had an especially crazy week.

More than anything, I craved a break from my harried life. I was sick of the domestic routine of picking up dirty towels, collecting random shoes strewn in every room, eyeing piles of folded clothes that never seemed to get put away. I was ready to take a deep breath and sip a martini. I was ready for a girls' night out. Who else to bring me back to my senses than my favorite fabulous females?

As I went through my contact list, I zeroed in on a few friends who always managed to lift me up when I was floundering and feeling like the worst mom, the worst wife, and the worst therapist. I envisioned a gathering that would feel like a party but be small enough for us to share our intimate stories, to let go of real life for an evening.

This being LA, I prepped for the evening the way I would for a special date with my husband, complete with false lashes and a fresh manicure, and my girlfriends did the same. I was the first to arrive, and I nursed an icy cold dirty martini at our table as my crew began to drift in, glammed up, accessorized from head to toe, and drawing admiring stares as they made their way through the crowded restaurant. We kissed and hugged and immediately launched into talk about vacations, our kids, and our recent retail-therapy expeditions. We doled out lavish compliments and laughed a lot.

But as the evening progressed and the buzz began to dissipate, a different rhythm took hold. My always-in-carpool-mode friend mentioned that she'd had a brush with death as she careened over two freeway lanes to avoid missing an exit. My attorney friend confessed that she was so drained after weeks of insanity at the office that she'd recently forgotten to file a motion. My single-mom friend, whose two-year-old still was not sleeping through the night, complained that she was constantly scatterbrained. Another girlfriend laughed sheepishly as she recounted the time we were chatting on the phone as she put the just-washed clean clothes from the dryer straight back into the washing machine! And for me, I told the group that the last book I'd downloaded on my Kindle was one I'd read a few months earlier and had completely forgotten about.

As we talked and sipped and vented and laughed and *kvetched,* it occurred to me that all of these silly but very real stories about life had everything to do with *mindlessness.* We were running from appointment to obligation to commitment to dinner to bed, only to start all over again. Truthfully, our lives were a blur. None of us ever seemed to stop moving long enough to notice any one thing, let alone appreciate it.

And we were the lucky ones. We had so much, more than we needed, yet all of us seemed to be missing that elusive trifecta: enough time, contentment, and gratitude.

I thought, *If we have all this and we're not satisfied, will we ever be?*

Once again, a girlfriend saved me. A few weeks later, my BFF, also a therapist, told me that she'd picked up a flyer for a mindful meditation retreat. "I want to go," she said, her eyes sparkling as she ticked off the benefits of mindfulness: how it could bring about calmness, reduce anxiety and depression, even help ease chronic pain. "I think you should go with me!" she said.

When I asked for details, she told me that it was essentially a day of meditation. A *silent* day of meditation. "I think it would do wonders for your anxiety," she said. That vague ennui and dread I've mentioned? I felt it pretty much from the moment I woke up until I turned in at night. It didn't matter if I tried to pay attention to it, figure it out, or ignore it—it was always with me, gnawing. Maybe mindful meditation could help me deal with it.

Still, I had my doubts. Could I really commit to sitting in a room, all day, and letting my mind go blank? And did I mention *no* talking? It sounded difficult, especially since I'd never meditated before. I had no idea, really, what mindful meditation was. I assumed that I had to chant or something, all while surrounded by hippie gurus. But my friend was up for it, and ultimately, I figured I'd better tag along. It was only eight hours—even I could manage that!

To my relief, the retreat actually involved much more than sitting silently in the lotus position with our eyes (and mouths) closed. I learned about the formal practice of mindful meditation, which involves sitting silently with the intention of noticing one thing (and knowing that you're noticing it). That one thing might be your breath, a physical sensation, or ambient sounds. Any one of these things can serve as an anchor, a focal point to which you can turn your attention when your mind starts to drift. It takes practice.

It sounds relatively simple, but it wasn't easy, as I discovered during the five formal meditations I sat through that day (each one lasting about twenty to forty minutes). At various times, I focused on my breathing, the sounds in the room, and yes, my feelings. I noticed the sun on my face and the shadows on the wall. During our silent meal, I noticed the crispy green salad on my plate and the awkward stares of the other participants. I also noticed my level of stillness and my heartbeat. It felt soothing. I felt present, blissful. All of it felt right.

I left the retreat feeling calmer, more focused, and knowing that I wanted to learn more about mindfulness, and even try meditating myself. If I could feel so different in a day, who knew what benefits I could reap if I really committed to mindful meditation over the long term? Maybe I'd found my own version of enlightenment! At the very least, I suspected I'd sleep better.

When I got home, I signed up for a weekly meditation class, which I still participate in. After seven years, each week still brings new insights. I've noticed my tendency to react too quickly to things I don't like. I can be judgmental toward myself and others. I have a tendency to ruminate over trivial things like my weight or obsess about what I might have done differently in my life. And the more I practice, the more I learn— and the less anxious I feel.

Since then, I have also become more comfortable with silence. I am a talker by nature, but I have discovered that quiet calms me down. I started seeking it out, noticing it. I appreciated moments when I didn't have to engage in small talk or fill an awkward pause with chatter; it felt like a liberation of sorts. My racing thoughts slowed and, yes, I slept better.

I also noticed that my meditation practice helped me become a better therapist. My clients mentioned how much calmer I seemed; they confessed that they felt more comfortable diving deeply into their stories and were less afraid of judgment (from me?). Perhaps that was because I was becoming a better listener, letting people find their words instead of rushing in with my thoughts.

During that entire first year of once- or twice-weekly meditating, I continued to notice subtle but powerful benefits. My best friend remarked on my new sense of calm, my metamorphosis from (slightly) neurotic Jewish mother to a kinder, gentler version of myself. It's not that I became someone else. I still resorted to the occasional bout of retail therapy, but I was happy with the parts of me that were emerging. I was changing, and I wasn't afraid to show it, especially with my loved ones.

It felt easier to be patient with my son (though not so much with math homework). When he was talking to me, instead of listening with half an ear as I checked my phone or computer, I found myself paying closer attention to his voice, his features, and his body language. I noticed that my husband had his own form of mindfulness practice out in our garden, where he creates beauty. I used to complain that his hobby, which consumed a chunk of the weekend, robbed us of his presence. Now I've come to appreciate that he pays attention to what he loves and nurtures it, much like he nurtures and provides for us. I am able to tell him how grateful I am for his hard and continuous work in caring for our family.

Inspired by the changes I noticed that first year, I began to seek out more mindful activities (daylong and weekend meditation retreats and a special seven-day yoga retreat to celebrate my fiftieth birthday). I also began reading books from notable Zen masters such as Thich Nhat Hanh, who writes about the concept of loving kindness as a power to bring about world peace. I read Jon Kabat-Zinn, founder of the eight-week Mindfulness-Based Stress Reduction program at the University of Massachusetts Medical Center, where patients with chronic pain have used mindfulness techniques to ease their suffering. I read Susan Albers, who writes about eating more mindfully, and Dr. Dan Siegel, who studies the impact of mindfulness on the brain. I found myself rereading Viktor Frankl's *Man's Search For Meaning*, knowing that I may have missed its deeper intimations when I read it the first time around in grad school.

The more I read, the more inspired I was to keep up my meditation practice. It took effort. I had to get out of my usual comfort zone and make conscious and deliberate decisions to get myself to every session. Sometimes, I'd notice my thoughts as I drove on the crowded 101 freeway to my weekly class (*This sucks! I think I'll just turn around and go back home!*), but I wouldn't give in to those thoughts. It's not that I dismissed them; in fact, I would acknowledge them and remember that

I had a different intention. I had a commitment that I wanted to keep. Sure, I could have come up with a dozen excuses to skip yoga or my meditation group, but the more I stuck with my deliberate intention, the more confident I became in other areas of my life. Saying that I would do these things and then actually doing them—despite the challenges and traffic jams—made me feel proud of myself. I was dedicated, which further fueled my determination. I felt like I was becoming my own cheerleader!

It has been more than seven years since I went on that first mindfulness retreat—and twenty years since that first women's weekend. There are now long stretches of time when I no longer feel anxious, no longer ruminate, and don't experience insomnia. More importantly, I feel more connected in all of my relationships. A few of my friends have even joined me in my weekly meditation practice. I continue to discover that my life, my *real* life, is happening every moment. Working, driving, shopping for groceries (and maybe a great handbag), making my bed, and brushing my teeth are all worth noticing, and with this noticing—the most basic form of mindfulness—comes calmness and a sense of freedom. What might happen in the future is anyone's guess. What has happened in the past cannot be changed. The only real change is how I choose to bring myself into everything I do—right now.

There is no *it* waiting to happen. This is *it*, complete with toothbrushing and laundry. To truly love my life, I have to notice these things, pause, and take in the details. The bliss comes in discrete moments, as I linger in a hot shower, savor my creamy homemade dressing, or even scrub a pot caked with last night's dinner. I appreciate being able to take my time as I fold the warm clothes from the dryer or the ebullient joy I experience when my son and I are in the car singing Pharrell's "Happy" at the top of our lungs. It turns out that there are infinite opportunities to notice and appreciate all the happy in my life. There always have been.

It may sound simplistic to say that noticing one's life is the key to happiness. But without inserting some kind of mindful and intentional practice into my day, life quickly reverts back to that blurry, frantic, angst-inducing autopilot routine. I'm here to tell you, girlfriend, that the blissful state you are hungry for is achievable by merely paying attention on purpose to the details and knowing you are truly experiencing them. Imagine that when your mom wants to spend an extra ten minutes on the phone, sharing the latest gossip from home, you are able to giggle along without rolling your eyes or counting the minutes, hoping for the call to end. Imagine the warmth and compassion your child will feel when you're not distracted by your cell phone as she recounts her fears of judgment from the other girls in her middle school. Imagine being present, being open, and listening without judgment or a need to fix. This is what mindfulness reaps.

You don't need to meditate daily (or even weekly) or take up yoga to get to this more mindful place. Sure, these formal practices can help, but if you're a busy woman like I am (and who isn't?), why not start with something simpler: taking notice of and loving the life you've already created?

I wrote this book to inspire you to notice the joy in your life instead of zeroing in on the negative or obsessing over things that are out of your control. Each chapter—one for every week of the year—will help you master simple techniques in listening, being compassionate, and appreciating your routine instead of feeling oppressed by it. The more you read, the more I think you'll be inspired to take a fresh approach to the most challenging things you encounter in work, love or, most important, within yourself, noticing all that is wonderful, moment by moment.

That's the gift of *Sitting Pretty*.

Week 1

A New Awakening

Let me give you an example of my typical Monday morning: Usually, I wake up without an alarm (yes, I'm a morning person!). When I'm not being mindful, within seconds, I'm heading to the bathroom to do my business while thinking about my husband, my son, my to-do list, my clients, what I want to eat, what I *should* eat, how much weight I gained this past weekend, whether I want to work out or go to yoga, what I'll write today, what errands I have to run, how my parents are feeling, and how tired I am—all this before I've even brushed my teeth!

Yes, in two to three minutes (or 180 seconds, max) I have run through the gamut of perpetual worries and obsessions in my head (I'm pretty sure that most of you, girlfriends, can relate to this). Often, these runaway thoughts leave me feeling anxious before I've even had my first sip of coffee, setting me up for a bummer day.

When I am being deliberately mindful, my day begins much differently. I wake up without an alarm and notice that I'm awake. I remain still for a few seconds, and then I carefully swing my legs over the side of the bed and rise. I know that I am doing this, though my mind may struggle a bit to focus. I'm aware of my internal resistance, my desire to just be on autopilot, but I intentionally stay present. I can feel my body in every movement, how my muscles tense and relax under my skin, how rested I am, the state of my mood. Notice, notice, notice. Check, check, check.

Next, I deliberately walk across the room, feeling the cushiness of the carpet under my bare toes. I stand for a moment, look out the window, and take in the sunrise—my favorite part of the morning. I stop and breathe. Then I proceed into the bathroom, noticing the different feel of the cool tiles against my bare soles, pausing for a moment, letting myself be still and balanced.

What distinguishes the first scenario from the second is simple awareness or noticing. I haven't done anything extra, haven't used up any more minutes, yet somehow, it feels as if I've gained time.

And you can do it too. Noticing in this deliberate way may seem overwhelming at first. You will likely find that your mind wants to do its own thing. But with continued practice, setting an intention of noticing your routine at the start of your day can have a tremendously positive impact on your mood and help you stay focused on the tasks ahead. Try it, and then observe how you feel. More energized, awake, present? There will be plenty of opportunities for your mind to wander, but if you can do just this one thing—first thing—you'll be amazed at how much clarity and optimism you can muster before that first cup of coffee.

Week 2

Brusha, Brusha, Brusha

Of all the mundane tasks in my day, I find brushing my teeth to be the most tedious. (Don't tell my hygienist.) Maybe it's because I rarely skip a session, and all that repetition makes it easy to be mindless rather than fully present and in the moment.

Think about it. Most of us brush our teeth 365 days a year, twice a day, for about two to three minutes a day—the length of time you need to sing the alphabet to yourself twice. I call that a devotion. When you repeat something that frequently, mindfully or not, you have created a ritual of sorts, one you can easily use as an anchor to start your day right.

Girlfriends, brushing your teeth is an opportunity to stop your mind from wandering or ruminating. It's important for your hygiene and for your overall physical health and well-being. Why not take the opportunity to apply mindful awareness to each step of the process, focusing your attention on the feel of your brush, the swirl of the soft bristles against your gums, and the taste of the toothpaste against your tongue? Take in a full, deep breath. Run your tongue slowly along your now-clean teeth. Stay present.

If your mind wanders, you can always bring your focus back to the task at hand without judgment. These few minutes are precious. There will be plenty of time for other thoughts or even obsessions. When you start going down that road, return to the present moment—even if it takes one hundred tries.

You can even look at brushing your teeth as a spiritual opportunity. Sounds crazy, right? But what if you considered this morning ritual a chance to brush away things you've said in anger or frustration, let go of yesterday's mindless words, and make way for those you have yet to speak? It casts a whole new light on the experience, doesn't it?

Week 3

Wake Up and Smell the Coffee. No, *Really* Smell It

What's your typical morning routine? Maybe you wake up at seven, slog out of bed (unless you're one of those energetic morning types like me), and eventually wend your way to the kitchen to make a pot of coffee. Or maybe you make your coffee on autopilot (sometimes I do too). But beneath the well-practiced motions—measuring, pouring, waiting, smelling the aroma, preparing my creamer, waiting some more for the beep of the machine to grant me the opportunity to enjoy my first cup of joe—I'm also aware that, with this routine, I am starting my day, a new beginning. If I am mindful, I know that this particular moment has never happened before—and it never will again.

Yes, I've made thousands of pots of coffee. Each morning, I awake in anticipation of that sip, letting the scent fill my nostrils, building anticipation of the caffeine buzz. Instead of rushing, I pour some half-and-half into my just-large-enough, chip-free, white porcelain mug and watch the swirl of the dark brew melding with the cream.

You may be saying to yourself right about now, "*Really?* Is that what I'm supposed to do every morning?"

Yes, that is precisely what I'm suggesting. Your morning routine is a perfect opportunity to adopt what's known as *beginner's mind*, which means approaching your usual tasks as if you've never done them before. In fact, you haven't.

Beginner's mind is a concept that brings you back to something familiar, like making a cup of coffee or commuting to work, except you consciously do those familiar things with a new openness or curiosity, without the preconceived thoughts and assumptions born of your prior experiences. When you adopt beginner's mind, you can feel that frisson of anticipation that comes with approaching something brand-new. To get to that place, you need to deliberately pay attention to each moment because each moment contains something unique. And once that moment is gone, it can't be recaptured or duplicated.

To be clear, I'm not asking you to deviate from your usual coffee- or tea-making except to pay close attention, on purpose, to this moment in your life. There's no need for you to add another item to your already-packed to-do list. You simply need to pay attention to what you're already doing, every single day.

Now, imagine looking at any of your other routine tasks the same way: making breakfast for yourself or for your family, feeding your pets, or reading the paper (do people still do that?). Whatever it is, when you wake up with a deliberate intention of bringing more awareness and clarity to your quotidian chores, moment by moment, you'll feel more conscious and grounded for the rest of your day.

It takes intention and commitment to move through your life this way, but I believe that it's worth it. Here at the beginning of your mindfulness journey, you will begin to see how simply paying attention to everyday tasks—*noticing* them—can lead to richer, deeper, and more meaningful experiences. Once you've experienced these simple activities more mindfully, you'll gain an entirely new appreciation for what you do and feel as you move through the world.

To make it easy for you, I'll lay it out step-by-step. Begin by paying deliberate attention to the details of your routine from the moment you wake up. Set out to do this for a few days, a week, or even a month, until you master it. You'll find that you become aware of colors, textures, fragrances, and tastes you may have been missing because you've been distracted and somewhat oblivious (checking Facebook or urging your kids to hurry up). That's what happens when you slip into mindlessness while going about the actions that comprise your life. The alternative is to notice everything and also to notice when you're *not* noticing. That's all there is to the practice of informal mindful meditation. And you can start right this minute. Doesn't that coffee smell heavenly?

Week 4

The LA Girl's Uniform

I don't think a day has gone by in my life in the burbs of Los Angeles that I haven't noticed a woman—or fifty—wearing black, Spandex-y, form-fitting yoga pants. I confess to wearing these cozies myself, mostly when I don't have to be in the office or when I'm back home after a long day at work or when I feel fat. In other words, I wear them most of the time.

Oh, I actually wear them to yoga too.

To me, the yoga-pant trend is an odd phenomenon. Years ago, these relaxed-knit pants were known as *sweatpants*. Now we've relabeled them to dignify our habit of wearing them outside the gym and often pay a fortune for that opportunity. Let's face it: the real reason we wear them is because they're more comfortable than jeans—and easier.

Bear with me while I ask you to consider this: You want to feel good about your body and yourself. You do what you can to keep up with your doctor's appointments, go to the gym, buy organic, take deep, calming breaths (and an intermittent Xanax), and attend the occasional yoga class.

But when did we all get so busy that we stopped making an effort to put our best self forward in everyday life? I think what we wear makes a difference. My bestie, for instance, does not wear her yoga pants every day. She only wears her yoga pants when she works out. I admire the time and effort she puts into her daily routine: doing her hair and makeup, selecting the appropriate outfit for her day, and finding the accessories to pull her unique look together. I love that she even *has a* look because it allows me to know her in a more intimate way. If you're thinking that she must have all the time in the world, think again. She simply makes putting her best self forward an intention.

What I'm suggesting here is that if you want to feel intimate and close to other people in your life, it helps to reveal yourself more expressively and individually—to go beyond yoga pants. Your personal appearance is an opportunity to be seen and experienced by even your closest friends in a new way. It takes deliberate effort, but not *too* much (we're not talking high maintenance here).

So, after your blissful cup of coffee, remind yourself of a few favorite pieces you haven't worn in a while, and how great they make you feel. Maybe it's that silky top you picked up at the mall or the new bra you got on sale at Victoria's Secret. Don't save these things for a special occasion. Wear them today and experience the pleasure they give you now. Then spend another minute finding the anti-wrinkle day cream with SPF 50+ you spent a fortune on and purposefully caress it into your beautiful face. Finally, pick out a sumptuous lipstick to match your mood—and you're good to go.

That, girlfriend, is called primping with intention, and it's another simple way to be mindful in your real life.

Week 5

Okay, So You Didn't Get out of Your Yoga Pants

What if you just can't bring yourself to put on your real clothes? Okay. After all, this book is about mindfulness, noticing the present, and staying with the flow. If you have your yoga pants on, you might as well consider … doing yoga. And not just any yoga. I should warn you that I'm one of *those* people who extol the virtues of Bikram or hot yoga. That's the one where you go into a 105-degree room, practice an open-eyed meditation for ninety minutes, and … *sweat!* I know, I know. I'm used to the resistance I get from my girlfriends when I urge them to join me. After all, who would willingly choose a workout in a too-close-for-comfort room filled with a bunch of sweaty people?

Bikram yoga can help you lose inches, improve your balance, strength, and flexibility, reduce the appearance of cellulite, and increase circulation and blood flow. All these things explain *my* primary motivation. That and the fact that yoga is actually considered to be a formal open-eyed meditation (as opposed to the informal practice of noticing that I've been talking about so far.) It involves practicing movements with intention and awareness. And I think it's just amazing because this kind of yoga practice can increase your ability to tolerate discomfort and "suffering."

I'm not implying that willingly shelling out money for a yoga class that makes you sweat is the equivalent of true suffering. I'm talking about suffering in the Buddhist sense, which means wishing that something were different in the moment. In Bikram yoga, suffering occurs when you are holding a position until your muscles scream. It involves barely being able to breathe while tolerating the heat. Suffering occurs when you're sure that everyone else is looking at you with judgment or when you try to hold a pose but your balance is off because your mind isn't really there. In the rest of life, suffering can show up as impatience, depression, anxiety, frustration, or ruminating—all things you'd prefer would disappear. Surprisingly, the more I practice Bikram yoga, the less I experience the other kind of suffering. My practice seems to teach me patience, non-judgment, and stillness, whatever the situation.

This is how it works: You've got ninety minutes to do twenty-six asanas (postures), stretching, breathing, reaching, and focusing while being led by a certified Bikram yoga instructor. The most important part is noticing your body and your mind and creating an intention for them to work together to complete each posture. As for the postures themselves, they are about balance, strength, focus, and training your attention on each part of your body so you can get into the posture and hold it.

Buried in the middle of the practice is a posture called *savasana* or corpse pose. It is not meant to be a break, a chance to lie down and relax. It is one of the twenty-six asanas, and it is just as important as the others—maybe even the *most* important. When done correctly, with intention, this pose—lying face up with your heels touching, arms close to your body—is the most efficient way to get yourself into a restful state. Deliberately bringing yourself to a quiet, resting position while breathing deeply and feeling the floor beneath you as you focus on your breath and the beating of your heart for two entire minutes teaches stillness in the midst of chaos. It can be heaven, especially after forty-five minutes of working your body to the max.

When you notice your mind telling your body to relax, you're honing a skill that can be used in your daily life. The more you practice, the greater your ability to use this skill when you need it most—whenever you're feeling upset or angry. With time, you'll be able to rely on your body to do as it's told, which is to be present, calm, and focused. And you'll suffer less.

Of course, Bikram also provides a kick-ass workout. But it isn't for everyone. The good news is that practicing *any* yoga can help you achieve a mind-body connection and leave you feeling more grounded and present.

You don't have to do yoga every day, but if you typically exercise at the gym and like to feel the burn, I highly encourage you to switch up your routine and include yoga—of any sort for a built-in mindfulness practice. If you can't get to a yoga studio, there are lots of options on YouTube and yoga instruction websites. But if you're as fortunate as I am and find a class you love, you might discover a community of like-minded girlfriends/yogis who will support and encourage you—and who even love to sweat with you.

Week 6

Take a Power Shower

My warm, steamy shower is one of the highlights of my day, especially after I get home from my yoga class, drenched in sweat. Even the anticipation on my five minute commute home feels like a sensual luxury, one I take very seriously, and not just because I'm a sucker for nice bath products. Here in Los Angeles, drought is a big problem, water is a luxury, and running a bubble bath or leaving the faucet on while brushing teeth is not something we do. So, taking a shower is a privilege for which I have immense gratitude.

Since I have only a few sacred moments for this ritual, I make a big deal out of it. I treat it as if it were a visit to a spa. First, I hold one of my favorite fluffy towels close to my cheek so that I can feel its softness, inhaling the lingering scent of my favorite laundry soap. It takes only a few seconds, but the effect of that pre-shower mindful pause can last all day. It slows me down and erases thoughts of what's coming next, what I have to do, or where I have to be. It creates space between now and the future.

When I can stay in the moment for the rest of the shower, the benefits continue, though I'll admit that I don't manage to do it daily. But mindfulness isn't about perfection. It's about noticing and continuous practice, which you can do anytime, anywhere. So try these steps (or just one) during your next shower to clear your head and experience a deeper sense of gratitude:

- Run the water and notice the initial droplets on your body. Some are warm, and some might still be chilly. Pause, then step directly into the center of the stream.
- Grab a loofah or a washcloth and start buffing with gentle, circular motions to wake up your skin, noticing the tingling sensations.
- Slowly and deliberately pour a small amount of shampoo into your palm and wash your hair carefully, massaging your head for a few heavenly seconds.
- Wash the rest of your body (to save water, try conditioning your hair simultaneously) and savor each sensation.

After my shower, I sometimes take a few seconds to reflect on how, by washing away grime and replacing it with cleanliness, I've create a new beginning. It can even be spiritual, or, at the least, a chance to be alone with my thoughts. Indeed, your shower may be the one time of day you have completely to yourself. Most women constantly wish for more time alone, so why not make the most of those moments of solitude when you actually have them? Why let yourself be consumed by any thoughts outside this exceptional moment?

Week 7

You've Got Stuff

As a therapist, I have noticed that most of us have issues with our stuff. Maybe you think you don't have *enough* stuff, and you believe that you've failed or that you're undeserving. Or maybe you envy those who do. At times, you may find yourself desperate for more or feeling confused and depressed when you're not sure you'll be able to get more.

On the other hand, maybe you think you have *too much* stuff and suffer shame, embarrassment, or guilt as a result. Or you accumulate items to prove to others (or to yourself) that you are truly successful.

Wherever you fall on this spectrum, obsessing about stuff can prevent you from noticing what it is you truly want. Contentment. Love. Security. And when you think about it, how you feel about your stuff reflects your relationships with almost everything and everyone in your life.

When I was younger and struggling to pay rent and bills, I went to seminars (thank you, Tony Robbins) and read books about how to feel empowered to create abundance in my life. I hoped that if I changed my thinking and could make myself believe *deep down* that I was more deserving of things like money and a good job, I would somehow attract these things into my life. There is some truth to this. You can manifest what you believe, but it wasn't until I began noticing and appreciating the present moment that I could feel love and gratitude for everything I already had.

Look around your home, your closet, or even your car: Are you able to notice and appreciate what you see? Do you feel love for your surroundings—or do you feel something else? Have you dusted off the little *tchotchke* you bought when you spontaneously stopped in at a cute store on a road trip, used the delicate wedding-gift teacups, or really looked at the painting you pass by in your hallway lately?

It's easy to let things become stand-ins for success, productivity, and self-worth or to let them become so familiar that you never see them at all. In fact, things are inanimate objects that can represent a time or place, an experience, or a connection.

Let me explain. There is one spot in my house that always inspires me and excites me. This may make me seem shallow, but the place where I really feel gratitude is inside my closet. I love my closet so much. In fact, I even meditate in there—on the floor! This closet—about ten feet by five feet—was built lovingly by my husband (who bequeathed it to me after I suggested that he use his office closet for his own clothes). It holds rows of shoes, purses, and clothes that I like to color coordinate for easy access. I have hats and scarves and pictures and posters displayed on the walls. There's also a cushy carpet covering the floor.

When I look around at all this, it's not just *stuff* I see. I see memories, gifts from friends and family, hard-earned items I purchased after much deliberation and consideration, and things I bought on a whim with friends. I see shoes I coveted and saved for, poster art with sayings that encourage and motivate me, and pretty sparkly things that excite me and bring out the girly-girl in me.

All that I believe to be true about myself is sitting in that closet, arrayed in front of me. I've arranged everything carefully, so I can take it all in. To the casual observer, it might look like a bunch of clothes, shoes, and purses, but when I take the time to notice it, to be mindful, it reminds me of the abundance and love I have in my life—and I feel so grateful.

Week 8

——— ✦ ———

The Spin Cycle

I have to admit that laundry is one household chore I actually enjoy. When the dirty clothes begin to pile up, I even feel a tiny sense of positive anticipation. (Call my crazy!) I wouldn't say that laundry is an exciting part of my day, but I do like the routine of separating the whites from the colors, checking pockets for tissues and change, and noticing and treating any stains. Sound strange? I don't think so.

If you look at laundry as a means of cleaning your clothes, and only that, you're missing an opportunity. There is an even greater gift here—one that arises from the details you might easily miss if you don't stop to notice them. It's true that laundry, with its series of repetitive actions, might feel like a difficult thing to truly focus on, especially when you have a lot on your mind. You're sorting colors and fabrics, digging into pockets, and attacking stains. So what? But these seemingly humdrum steps offer an opportunity to practice mindful awareness by putting deliberate attention into each and every part of the ritual.

Why bother? Well, if you can connect laundry (or any other chore) with a sense of purpose, you can transform it from a dreaded task into something that makes you feel good about yourself. One way to do that is to think about how your family (or you) need and enjoy having clean clothes (even if certain people in your life don't always realize it). The more you reflect on that, the less resentful you'll likely feel about the task. In my counseling practice, I've learned that when people feel they have purpose, their self-esteem and sense of personal power increases. I have experienced this myself. And yes—you can get this purpose from something as trivial as laundry.

So, today—or whenever you next put in a load—think of it as an exercise in building self-esteem and patience. You're fulfilling an obligation, sure, but it's an obligation that reflects your commitment and care. Clothes cover your body, but they are also an expression of your style, of who you are. By taking care of them, you are, in a way, showing a bit of reverence for them, reverence for yourself.

As you sift through your basket of dirties, look at each item and think about it for a few seconds: Where did it come from? Who made it? Did a person weave the fabric and sew the seams, or did a machine sew it up? If you notice a grass stain on your son or daughter's top, imagine your child sliding across the lawn in giggles. When you pluck out a dollar bill from the pocket of your favorite jeans, take a moment to remember when you placed it there.

Next, carefully, separate the clothes into two piles—light and dark. Notice the different shades of dye, the weight of each garment, the texture, and even the smell of sweat! Shake each piece out and hold it at arm's length, noticing your actions. Carefully inspect these items as you think about the care you are putting into this task at this moment.

Now it's time to decide which setting to use on the washer. Notice if you have a load small enough for a quick-wash setting. These things matter—simple attention to details like these can help the environment and save time.

Measure out your detergent carefully and then listen to the sound of the washer door clicking shut. Watch for the cycle to start before rushing off to your other chores, noticing when you'll have to return to transfer clothes to the dryer. As that time approaches, pay attention to any feelings of anticipation.

When you're ready to remove your wet clothes, open the door gently. Carefully begin removing the items and observe yourself doing this task deliberately, with patience.

Try to be gentle as you untangle pants and bra straps. Think about which clothes you intend to hang dry, set them aside, and then toss the rest into the dryer. Pick your setting and start the cycle, noticing the turn of a dial or press of a button.

When your clothes are ready, carefully remove each item, piece by piece, taking in the warmth from the dryer. Do your folding immediately, so that the clothes you've carefully tended to don't wind up in a messy, wrinkled stack. As you carefully crease your T-shirts and fold your sheets, think about how these items are now clean, fresh, and neat. Feel the satisfaction that comes with knowing you've paid attention and done a task well.

These steps may seem laborious or even trivial, but I think you'll discover that doing laundry with attention—and intention—doesn't eat up many extra minutes. Instead, it creates an opportunity to practice patience and place your focus on just one thing during an otherwise whirlwind day. You'll discover that, in the ninety minutes or so you've spent washing and drying your clothes, you've connected with your life in a deliberate, patient, and calm way.

Week 9

=== ❦ ===

Cross Stress off Your To-Do List

About twenty years ago, I had an epiphany. It was not the sudden kind—it was more subtle than that, a tiny realization that shifted my thinking about everything. I realized that if I looked at my everyday activities as just a bunch of crap I had to do before I could get to my *real* life, then most of my life was actually made of crap. Fact is, up until that moment, I didn't recognize that my take on pretty much everything I did was negative, that I considered my real life full of crap I had to do. Ugh. Not a good insight.

Once I became more mindful and learned how to pay attention on purpose, I started hearing my inner tone of voice—really *hearing* it. I discovered that the insidious negative self-talk started as soon as I woke up (*I wish I could stay in bed!*), during my morning routine (*Ugh. I don't feel like shaving my legs*), when I got into my car to go to work (*I hope the traffic doesn't suck!*), and when I came home (*Another pile of laundry and dishes! I'm so bored!*). I caught the negative messages when I went back to the store for a forgotten ingredient (*Crap!*) and when I cleaned up after dinner (*Double crap!*). The more I noticed what I was saying to myself, the clearer it was how rarely I felt grateful for these moments. Instead, I felt oppressed by them.

Yet, the life I've just described is the life most of us lead. If we choose to call it boring because of the repetition or annoying because it's not pleasurable every moment, we will eventually resent every bit of it and want something else. But there *is* nothing else. Every life is made up of some mundane moments, which is why, to be content, it's crucial to live fully in the life you already have, accepting your responsibilities and moving through them with as much grace as possible.

In other words, I had to change my outlook and make a conscious, deliberate change in the way I talked to myself and approached my life, starting with my chore list. Instead of telling myself I had so much crap to do, the first thing I did was change the word *crap* to *stuff*, a more palatable and benign term, an attempt to remove the *suffering* from my daily experience. Immediately, I noticed that my attitude toward these mundane tasks didn't feel quite so oppressive. Attitude is everything.

By creating a different, more positive association around each of your necessary tasks—tasks you might previously have thought of as annoying—it's possible to feel more engaged and purposeful toward each of them. That's when the contempt will fall away. If you are fully present while completing your ordinary obligations, you have an opportunity to see new meaning in them, and maybe, just maybe, enjoy them.

I know you're catching my message here: When you fully accept your life as a series of obligations, commitments, and responsibilities and engage in them instead of wishing them away, you have a chance to approach each of these things in a deliberate, gentle, and curious manner. That's when you'll actually feel joy—not just when your chores are over but also while you're in the midst of them.

Week 10

Help. Get Me out of Here!

Have you ever found yourself spending time on the phone or having lunch or coffee with a friend when you suddenly notice that your mind has drifted and you're not really listening? Sure, you're there, but you're not really there *there*. Yes, you can sum up what you've heard, but you're not engaged, maybe because it has been fifteen or twenty minutes and your friend hasn't come up for air. She's simply droning on and on and on about her job, kids, husband, and stress.

During those moments, I find myself reflecting on what I really want (and need) from people I choose to spend time with. I want to feel connected. After all, I did make the choice to be there, whether or not the experience turns out to be satisfying. My meditation teacher says, "You're not having the experience you want—you're having the experience that you're having." Suffering comes from wanting something you don't have. To reduce suffering, you've got to be engaged in the experience you're having.

Maybe if I told my friend that I've noticed that she has a lot on her plate, then inserted a comment or story about my life into the conversation, I could shift things a bit. But what I have found is that listening—truly engaging in the conversation, even if I have to stop the train for a few moments to check in with comments like, "Wow, that must have been difficult," or "Sounds like you're under a lot of pressure," or "I noticed that this happens to you a lot"—can jolt my friend into remembering that there's another person here, and that I really do care. Yes, I do.

Of course, that's not a guarantee that she'll stop or slow down enough to ask how you're doing. When you're caught in a situation where you're not feeling heard or seen, there are a few things you can do. The first is to stop checking out and drifting off—and start tuning in. This focus shifts your mind from wondering when it's your turn to talk to focusing on listening and being present. Another way to create more connection is to be honest and straightforward about what you are feeling (tactfully). You might say, "I love getting together with you, and it seems like we always need more time so that we can both share what's been happening in our lives … There's so much going on that these lunches fly by without really getting a chance to connect. That's what I was really looking forward to when we made our plans." Okay, so that may sound a little scary to some of you (it did for me when I first tried it), but I have found that taking the risk of openly and honestly communicating your feelings to a true friend can lead to a more fulfilling relationship.

Of course, if these approaches fail, it may be time to reflect on what your friend really offers you. Connection is a two-way street, but not all relationships must be 100 percent reciprocal. Maybe she offers the occasional good laugh or a shared love of music, and that's it.

It's easier to realize that if, when you're with a friend and find yourself drifting and imagining a day alone at the beach instead, you stop to take her in, listen carefully, and read between the lines. If the friendship is worth it, you'll know what to do.

Week 11

Don't Just Do Something ...
Sit There!

It's not too often that I find myself with a bunch of free time in the middle of my day, but when I do, I rarely savor it. Instead, I've gotten into the bad habit of logging onto my Facebook page and toggling between photos of my friends' latest vacations ("Like!"), e-mail, and the occasional text.

Yes, I do this stuff too. I never feel good about it because, in the back of my mind, I know I'm missing something. It's called *life!* I know this even as I open another tab or app to play a game or browse the headlines.

What would happen if, during those unexpected moments of free time, I did absolutely nothing except notice? Think about it: When was the last time you stood in line at the grocery store without reaching for your phone? For most of us, it has become nearly impossible to stay still and silent. Instead, we assuage our anxiety by distracting ourselves with our gadgets.

Despite my Facebook habit, I've spent a lot of time learning to value stillness and quiet. It hasn't come easily. The first time I remember acknowledging how tough it was for me to simply *be* in a space without activity or chatter was during my first silent meditation retreat. We were asked to refrain from speaking—even during meals. The intention was to begin to notice ourselves, fully, rather than engaging in small talk.

Except what I noticed, at least at first, was the awkwardness of it all. I didn't have a lot of practice simply being with people and not talking.

Tough as it was, it turned out to be a great exercise in becoming aware of my inner state rather than what was happening all around me. I noticed the freedom that came from not having to do the socially acceptable thing, aka make small talk with strangers.

I also noticed that my mind wandered, a lot. I noticed that the color on the walls looked different across the room. I noticed that others around me became less fidgety during the course of the day. I noticed that I felt as if I were part of some gigantic organism in a room full of breathing souls. (Yes, really.) I noticed that I was smiling.

This was not a formal meditation. All I was doing was heeding an instruction to not speak (or text or e-mail) throughout the day. But the experience was different enough that it affected me from then on. I realized that *busyness* has been redefined to mean *productive*—even when it's not. In that way, we've made constant busyness acceptable in a way that silence and stillness are not.

For the past seven years, I've been lucky enough to live only fifteen minutes from the gorgeous beaches of Malibu. Before that, it took me more than an hour to reach them, so I never went. Yet I always longed for a getaway, thinking I needed to hop on a plane to disconnect. It wasn't until a few years ago that I began to take advantage of my proximity to the beach and avail myself of hour-long staycations during otherwise frenetic days.

It has become a deliberate choice to leave a beach blanket in my car in case I have the opportunity to steal away for a few hours by myself. I notice that I feel almost embarrassed if I tell my girlfriends that I went to the beach for an hour before picking up my son from school, lest they judge me for being lazy or hedonistic. But another part of me is please and proud of myself, for my ability to make stillness and quiet a priority in my life. I am grateful that I live only fifteen minutes from the beach, but I think that if a park or pond were nearby, I'd still seek out solitude.

Sometimes, I get the stillness I crave by doing random chores without music, reveling in the silence. I used to need the music to make my chores feel more fun; now I take pleasure in the calmness I feel when I let some quiet into my life. Later, when I'm stirring a pot of soup or wiping down the bathroom sink, the benefits, the calmness, seem to linger, slowing me down, yet energizing me.

To bring more peacefulness into your life, you must learn to tolerate stillness and quiet. Think you don't have time for these moments in your life? The next time you realize you've been binge-watching Netflix or distracting yourself with your mobile device while standing in line at Starbucks, *stop*. Put down your phone. Breathe. Be still. Take in this moment of silence and feel the calmness enveloping you. It takes a certain kind of courage to step away from your phone or computer, with the intention of doing absolutely nothing but noticing. But the more you insert these moments of quiet into the nooks and crannies of your day, the more exhilarated you'll feel.

Week 12

Time for a Walkabout

One of my lovely girlfriends got me thinking the other day. We were talking about our routines, and she mentioned how she tries to walk every chance she gets. Where I live, this is radical thinking.

LA is not a walking city. We drive down the street for a cup of coffee and on the freeway to work. Often, we Angelenos sit in our car for hours at a time. When I moved here from the East coast, I was shocked and awed by the car culture. Everyone loves their cars: the make, model, and year are things people actually know and recite when asked (and even when they're not).

I quickly got into the car culture myself. I loved that the first time I went to the grocery store, on the West side, there was free valet parking! I think I had a good long laugh about that! I was definitely not used to being pampered in this way, but I quickly adapted to this luxury.

I'd go out to lunch and valet my car. I'd go to a restaurant and valet my car. I could even go to a certain dry cleaner and valet my car! Soon enough, this became a little game. I'd actually pass on establishments without a valet to avoid the extra one-minute walk to reach the door of my destination.

When my East Coast friends began to make fun of me, I stopped that nonsense. I found parking spaces like the rest of the world and moved on. Of course, I still love a valet when I'm dressed in my four-inch heels, but otherwise, I've learned that because of where I live, I have to remind my body to move.

Going to the gym is one thing. It satisfies my physical urge to keep my body healthy (and yes, it helps me feel as though I can keep up in the land of the beautiful people.) My workouts also assuage some of my guilt if I've indulged in extra calories over the weekend.

Taking a walk is another thing all together.

I'm talking about a quiet walk with no music, no phone calls or texting, and no distractions. Just simply taking deliberate steps, feeling the ground beneath my feet, stopping to admire a neighbor's bougainvillea, smelling the orange blossoms, and feeling *alive*. Actually, *noticing* that I'm alive.

I think of this kind of walk as an informal meditation. Like all meditations, it brings my attention to the present moment and creates a space where I can get centered and calm.

Unlike the walks I take for exercise, where I drown out my thoughts with loud dance music that propels me to stride faster, when I take a walk for the pleasure of enjoying some alone time and noticing the world around me, I leave my headphones at home and purposefully try to spot something new—even on a route I've traversed hundreds of times. I adopt beginner's mind, looking at the world in a fresh, new way.

My walks begin with deliberately choosing to stay present from the moment I leave my front door to the moment I return. Staying present, for me, means focusing on whatever I see, hear, or smell during my walk. When my mind drifts—and it does—I gently nudge it back to this intention, to noticing the beautiful space surrounding me.

Try it. Leave your car behind. Think about the direction in which you want to go, notice the way your feet feel in your sneakers, and stand still for a moment. Take in the birds singing, the leaves on the trees, the sky, and the daytime moon. Feel grateful.

Week 13

What Did You Just Say?

We tell ourselves horrible things. Yes, really, we do. We call ourselves *fat pigs* when we don't fit into our jeans, *stupid idiot* if we make silly mistakes, or *ditz* when we can't remember an acquaintance's name.

Sometimes this kind of negative self-talk feels incessant. We wake up and begin the day by getting on the scale, then let the number dictate our mood or define our self-worth. We decide if it's a good day or a bad day based on a moment of time during which we've chosen to inflict pain on ourselves.

I won't get into the *why* of it here. I'll just say that we should all notice it—and *stop it!*

I'm being a bit dramatic, but I'm certain that, at one time or another, most of us have made life decisions based on self-recrimination. Need an example? How about not going on an interview because you didn't think you were smart enough for the job? Or skipping the beach (or a family party) because you'd gained five pounds? Or what about not writing that book because you're not a "real" writer?

I first noticed this habit in myself some time ago when a girlfriend commented on how I had a tendency to say (out loud), "I'm so stupid!" whenever I messed something up. She started calling me on it, telling me that I'd just done it again. Once she started pointing it out, I was shocked at how often those harsh words came out of my mouth.

Did I really believe I was stupid? Maybe a part of me did. And maybe that's why I wasn't all that happy with my life—in that stuck place I mentioned earlier.

Your decisions reflect how you perceive yourself, and too often, that perception is shaped by a snarky inner voice, the voice that tells you that you are stupid, not good enough, or flabby. But the truth is that you can use self-talk to convince yourself of just about anything. So why not use it for good?

I'm talking about noticing again—of becoming mindfully aware of what you tell yourself about yourself. Once you begin paying attention, it's likely that you'll make an effort to be a bit kinder, which will make you feel more confident and give you the space to become more creative and successful.

This girlfriend and I ended up devising a strategy to silence our negative inner voices—a strategy I still use today. Whenever I catch myself in the middle of a defeatist statement, I purposely say *delete, delete, delete*—aloud—removing the bad words from my mind while visualizing my finger pressing the backwards-arrow key on an IBM Selectric typewriter (yes, I'm dating myself). It might sound crazy, but the technique helps shut down the self-critical, judgmental voice inside of me.

I really want to help you out with this one. I'll admit—it's a toughie. That is why, if this is a challenge you are prepared to take on, I strongly encourage you to enroll your girlfriends to help you out. They'll notice the negativity even when you don't.

First, pick a mantra or a slogan or something to visualize, *anything* that will stop you in your tracks when you start walking down the road of self-abuse. You can even write a positive message in big, bold lipstick letters across your bathroom mirror—a phrase that evokes a feeling of self-worth that takes a sledgehammer to your inner critic.

As the days pass and you make an effort to speak more gently to yourself, notice how your own perception of who you are changes. It will be different, for sure. Imagine how your friends, your child, your partner, your boss, or even your local barista might begin to see you—as a strong, confident, capable woman. Everyone else already knows that you're amazing. It's time for you to see it too.

Week 14

How to Make a Bad Day Better

Ever have one of those mornings when, for no apparent reason, you wake up slightly anxious or sad or just feeling *off*? You wish you didn't have to walk the dog, get dressed, go to work, do errands, drive the carpool, or be responsible. You're not up for it.

Somehow, you actually manage to get up, get dressed, and go to work because it's your life—and you can't just quit. People are counting on you. Since you are dependable and trustworthy, you move forward, whatever your mood.

I'm here to tell you that *sometimes* you can stay in bed. Yes, it's really okay to not do anything but pay attention to that weird mood and respond by being gentle with yourself. When I say *gentle,* I mean careful, attentive, and temperate. Think of these moods as an opportunity to look carefully and notice your life. You don't have your usual oomph. Okay, fine. No need to analyze, ruminate, obsess, or worry. You're human, and you're not always going to be on. What you *can* do is take a step back from your busy, overscheduled life and pause.

When I get into this kind of funk, I try not to overthink it. Instead, I notice it. I feel a little sad, a little bored of my routine. If I just wait, stay mindful, and simply notice myself, eventually, my mood changes, because everything changes. But in the moment, I have no idea how long that will last. So I decide to do something different. Not hugely different, but different nonetheless.

I'm not saying that it's okay to drop everything and hide under the

30

covers or ignore your pet (or your kid). That would cause more anxiety! What I am saying is that for one day, you don't have to fuss over the dishes in the sink. I'm saying that the laundry can wait for twenty-four hours and so can a shower. One of my favorite things to do differently is to browse my old family photos. I may notice something I haven't seen the previous hundred times. If I'm reminded of a faraway friend, I may call her.

I also like to get a little creative. I keep a stack of sharpened colored pencils in a container on my desk in case I have the urge to doodle for ten or fifteen minutes. Drawing lines and circles helps me stay focused and, strangely, brings me enormous pleasure.

You don't have to doodle. Any deliberate effort you make toward something that brings you joy is a good thing, especially during those blah moments in life. You may find that singing into your hairbrush at the top of your lungs while dancing to Madonna does the trick. I say go for it.

Week 15

🐝

Making an Entrance

Grrr ... umph ... snarl ... sniff, sniff ... oh, shit! Cough, cough, rustle, rustle.
All this in the past *minute* while I listen as I stand in line for my latte.

How about the person who bursts into a quiet room in full, loud conversation with a friend and fails to notice that everyone is looking at her (and not with happy expressions)? What about when you're at a restaurant and are trying to talk to your dining partner, but you can't concentrate because you can hear every word the lady in the next booth is saying—every detail of her phone conversation, in which she is describing, loudly, her latest crazy blind date? What about when you and a friend are talking to each other during a concert or a play, despite the dirty looks of your husband, among others? Oops, that last one was me.

What I'm suggesting here is that you might want to consider treading lightly, being just a tad more aware of your presence and impact on a space (especially when entering it). Take a moment and pause to assess the playing field. It's important to be mindful of how your presence impacts everyone else.

This is something I've worked on improving. Some people seem to know this kind of thing intuitively, and others were clearly schooled growing up. They know not to put their elbows on the table or run though the china department at Macy's, but some may have missed that lesson.

I'm not just talking about having good manners or proper etiquette, though what I'm saying is related to that. I would put it into a category of awareness. When you are aware of yourself in any given situation, you're better able to make some accommodations based on what others may be expecting. And when you're aware, you become part of something rather than being separate and oblivious.

A few years ago, my husband and I were enjoying a bit of R & R at a lovely hotel for our anniversary. We were jazzed to have some alone time, just being together in the same space, enjoying the calm and each other's company. The pool area happened to be pretty crowded, but we were seated at the far end near the entrance to a Japanese garden—an ideal spot to camp out for a few hours.

Except soon after we'd settled ourselves in our lounge chairs, a large night-after-the-wedding party of twenty-somethings casually and loudly took up positions immediately adjacent to my chair, chitchatting and laughing loudly. I don't normally think of myself as a buzzkill, but their sheer lack of awareness of space was mind-boggling. Didn't they notice that most of the other guests were relaxing, or quietly reading? Or, better yet, couldn't they have the foresight to plan something more appropriate, like hanging out at the hotel bar? Didn't they notice the venomous stares and eye-rolls in their direction?

All it takes is noticing the sounds emanating from your mouth or your body and the attitudes and reactions of those around you. A quick look will let you know if you are doing the right thing in the right place at the right time or if you need to make an adjustment. When you're mindful of the space you're sharing, you'll benefit—and so will everyone else.

Week 16

Unsocial Media

Imagine that it's your birthday. You're sitting at your computer or holding your smartphone and scanning your Facebook page. Your heart is racing, your mouse is scrolling, and you're feeling elated that all of your "friends" thought of you today. It's a good feeling, but is it borne out of true, thoughtful friendships? Or is Facebook simply a lazy way of staying connected?

Like you, I get caught up in the high of Facebook and other social media, liking my friends' posts, reading about their "amazing" lives, and looking at their family photos and the delicious meals they're consuming. The trouble comes when I use this habit as a substitute for what I really want, which is knowing others and being known. While I may get a temporary buzz when people respond to my online posts, an actual real-life connection is what truly fills me with joy.

We used to feel this instinctively. I still remember growing up, biding my time as my older sister hogged the phone in the kitchen. She'd pull the coiled cord as far as it would go, away from listening ears, chatting with her girlfriends, laughing and whispering for hours. Sometimes, she was on the phone for so long that if someone were trying to reach us, they'd have to use an emergency breakthrough from the phone company! We didn't have call waiting back then or cell phones, but even as I lurked and gave her the stink-eye, I felt that something special and important was being discussed, and it belonged only to her.

Eventually, I got a bit older and spent my own time on the phone, talking and whispering and laughing. Just a short while back, my high school bestie called me with her teenaged daughter in the car to tell me how she was reminded of when we would talk about boys and our silly adolescent adventures. We used to laugh so hard we'd actually pee our pants! I smiled all day after that call. It warmed my heart to know that some memories—and true friendship—could still bring me such enormous pleasure.

Research shows that the more devices people acquire to stay connected, the more alone they feel. Technology isn't totally to blame for that loneliness. If you want to maintain your close relationships, you need to make a deliberate choice to stay connected. That can be as simple as sending an e-mail or a text, though I believe that to truly *know* another person, you have to make time for a personal interaction through a phone call or a face-to-face conversation. Reaching out to call someone is a mindful act of love and kindness that requires empathy, compassion, listening, and being present. In contrast, mindlessly and habitually trolling social media reinforces the false belief that with each like, we are actually getting what we want: connection. The truth is that all those likes keep us disconnected from our true intentions.

Over the years, I've learned as a therapist and as a friend that isolation from others feeds sadness, anxiety, and worry. Social media defeats the purpose of the very human desire to be seen and heard. It's about immediate gratification. Press a button, and you're "connected"— kind of. I also know that when I reach for the phone to call a friend or my mom, it's the listening and laughing that brings me real joy.

Week 17

Slow Down, You're Moving Too Fast

The other day, I decided I wanted to browse though my iPhoto library. After setting myself up with a tall glass of water and Ed Sheeran on Pandora, I glanced at the bottom bar in search of the little iPhoto icon, only to realize it wasn't there. In its place was a little flower thingy. I clicked on it with trepidation.

Immediately, I was taken through a tutorial that was supposed to teach me how to access my photos and projects. Except when I tried to maneuver through the new application on my own, I discovered I couldn't find my photos. The message read: *Insufficient storage space.* I freaked. I immediately started sifting through my computer files, but I couldn't find my photos anywhere.

If only I had paid attention and slowed down while downloading my latest OS update instead of clicking accept (my autopilot habit), that afternoon of panic would never have happened.

I finally found my photos, but the experience made me wonder how many of us rush through stuff to get to the next set of stuff only to end up in a mess we could have avoided, whether lost eyeglasses, technical snafus, or double-booked appointments. When I find myself making those kinds of mistakes, I know I need to just take it easy. I need to slow down and notice what I'm doing. Paying mindful attention to the task at hand is such a simple notion, yet it's not easy to do.

Take texting as an example. It used to be that I would type a text quickly and the darned autocorrect would find some crazy replacement for my thought. Then, I would send another message to correct the autocorrect, and it would replace the wrong word with yet another wrong word. If only I'd slowed down long enough to look at the incorrect text in the first place, I'd have saved myself a minute—and much more than that in frustration (not to mention the frustration of my friend on the receiving end of the garbled text).

My BFF calls me Speedy Gonzales, an endearing term that refers to my tendency to go about most of my tasks and plans as if my pants were on fire. She has pointed out that it would behoove me to slow down and read that last e-mail so that I actually catch the details (instead of making assumptions). When faced with a string of e-mails between friends, my usual MO is to skip-read and then quickly answer what I assume is the question. Often, I'll answer incorrectly, and wind up making the entire e-mail chain even more confusing. Of course, a single phone call could eliminate the confusion, but reading with my full attention would also nix the problem.

The results of not paying attention, wholeheartedly, can be worse than a bungled e-mail. Once, while preparing for a dinner party, I was flying through my to-do list only to find my thumb bleeding profusely from a misaimed knife while slicing into a butternut squash. If you've ever prepared butternut squash, you probably know that it's one vegetable that needs your wholehearted attention. The butternut squash incident taught me to be present and deliberate when handling a knife—and more.

We all want to be productive, get stuff done, and move on, but paying deliberate attention and completing one thing at a time helps you avoid making mistakes, both large and small. Worth it? I'm sure of it.

Week 18

Doodling Away

Some of you may scoff at the idea that you have the ability to create any type of art—that you might be able to draw, paint, or sculpt. Maybe you think you lack talent. Hmm.

If you can draw a straight line or a circle, you've started something. That's what I tell myself as I pursue my intention to become more creative, which includes writing, journaling, doodling, and, most recently, Zentangling. Zentangle® is a meditative art form that starts with a pattern of lines and circles that evolve into an expression of creativity. It was invented by Rick Roberts and Mary Thomas (find out more at http://www.zentangle.com), and it involves drawing images with black pen on white paper tiles or squares, a process that reduces stress and increases focus and motivation. Each drawing or image includes symbols, designs, and patterns taken from numerous cultures, but the design that emerges from the various lines and shapes is always unique and surprising. You can learn to do it with simple tutorials on YouTube, find samples on Pinterest, or go to your local arts and crafts store for a book on the technique.

I started Tangling after noticing an incredible white pumpkin that my friend, Holly, was decorating for Halloween. As we were waiting for our yoga class to fill up, she quietly proceeded to doodle little lines and circles in a neat formation that became a unique and interesting piece. Check out the photo of her pumpkin below.

I was immediately curious. She told me that she had recently been certified as a teacher in this technique and invited me to participate in one of her classes at a local craft store. That's all the motivation I needed to begin my creative journey.

The best thing about it is that anyone can do it—regardless of artistic talent. When it comes to things like drawing and painting, it's easy to let self-judgment and criticism snuff out any effort or exploration. Sometimes you need to challenge your resistance and prove your self-doubt wrong.

One thing I like about Zentangling is that by using a pen instead of a pencil, you're forced to incorporate any mistakes into your pattern (no erasing!) The "mistakes" become reminders to stay present and return your focus to the pattern you're creating. Knowing that there's no final picture to be judged is actually quite liberating.

Zentangle® is, in fact, a form of meditation. It requires that you sustain your attention and focus without judgment. Do this doodling for a while, and you'll discover a certain rhythm to the process. Thich Nhat Han says that we should strive for aimlessness in life rather than continually striving to be number one. Zentangling promotes this type of aimless experience, one that, ironically, will help you stay focused on the present moment rather than worrying about the future. Since there is no expected outcome, all that's left is to enjoy the process.

Holly's designs:

My designs:

Week 19

§

Driving While Applying Makeup

You're stuck in slowly crawling traffic (or I am—welcome to life in LA!). *Why not make good use of my time?* You manage to pull out your makeup bag and rummage around for the eyeliner and mascara, the lip liner and lipstick. You pull down the visor mirror, and with one eye on the road and a hand on the steering wheel (or your thigh on the steering wheel), you manage, barely, to do a decent job of putting on your face.

We all know that it's not cool to do this while driving, yet somehow, we continue to let ourselves get distracted behind the wheel. Some of us apply makeup, some send texts, others eat their breakfast, and some actually read the paper (I've seen this!) Mindful driving, it isn't.

In contrast, remember when you first took the wheel, at sixteen or seventeen, and your parents and teachers coached you to pay close attention to every detail? Buckle your seatbelt. Adjust the mirrors and seat. Make sure your turn signal is on. Look around for pedestrians before pulling away from the curb.

I remember my very first solo drive in my parents' 1973 green Plymouth Duster. I was so excited to finally have my new license in hand, and my first trip was straight to my boyfriend's house. I was nervous and exhilarated! Still, I was extremely careful to use my turn signals, stop at all the stop signs, and keep the radio off so I could give this new experience my full attention. All of this happened more than three decades ago, yet I vividly remember the excitement of the moment—how profoundly this milestone weighed on me.

So, what happened? Well, as with many things we do daily, hourly or weekly, conscious awareness gradually recedes, and we begin acting on autopilot, anticipating the feeling and experience of getting into a vehicle and starting the engine without focusing on it. We know how long our driveway is and how many seconds it will take to back out of the garage. We reflexively adjust our mirrors. All of this still on autopilot.

However long you've been driving, it's possible to approach the experience with a beginner's mind. It's another opportunity to practice mindfulness in your everyday routine, except that this one can actually be a lifesaver. When you hear of a young person hit by a distracted driver or a family destroyed by someone's inattentiveness, it's all too easy to judge and admonish. It's important for all of us to take responsibility for staying focused and in a state of constant noticing behind the wheel.

Before you reach for the keys, stop. Think. Where are you going? What road will you travel? What will you pass? I urge you to notice the feel of the wheel, your hands at ten and two. Can you sense the texture of the road under your wheels? I implore you to notice the faces of the passengers in your rearview mirror, using your full capacity to pay attention. I'd like you to appreciate the gravity of the moment. After all, each moment is uniquely different—and driving is no exception.

Week 20

On the Menu: Everything That's Not Nailed Down

The other night, I had a moment of feeling overwhelmed. It happens occasionally. I reacted, as I often do, by having a mini binge fest—a small Twix chocolate bar, some salty crackers, a little orange, a handful of almonds, and those delectable veggie chips. *Yum.* Yet, in the middle of chewing and swallowing, I suddenly felt that something was very wrong.

I was sitting on my sofa, watching some movie I'd already seen, reaching for the aforementioned not-too-bad-for-me Trader Joe's chips, shoveling the yummy little salty-crunchy morsels into my mouth. My hand was bobbing in and out of the bag as if attached to a synchronized robotic arm. My mind was not conscious of this action (nor was I paying much attention to the movie) until my stomach started screaming at me to stop.

I stopped.

One bag of junk food was almost gone (not to mention the Twix bar, crackers, orange, and almonds). I should have been proud that I stopped. At least I'd finally noticed that my hand-to-mouth action was out of control. Instead, I felt angry with myself and ashamed. I went to bed feeling a little worried that I must have some sort of eating disorder! (I know—a bit neurotic.) I'm not the first person to open a bag of chips (or a box of Girl Scout cookies) and make the contents disappear. It's just that sometimes, when I catch myself doing it, my mind gets away from me. I begin to ruminate on this terrible habit that leaves me feeling miserable.

The next morning, the misery continued. I spent some time overanalyzing what was going on in my life. My computer was on the fritz, my volunteer job was taking up too much of my time, my writing deadlines were scaring me, and my son had just notified me of a school project was due the next day—and he hadn't even started it. All normal stuff, yet I was almost over the edge.

When I approach that precipice, I binge eat. I don't fall over into the abyss too often, but when I do, it's like a sledgehammer that comes down quickly, pounding me emotionally and physically.

The only antidote I've found is empathy— the ability to share and understand the feelings of another. For me, empathy toward myself is the antidote to my crazy, out-of-control behavior. When I can vent or say things aloud, I almost always get a new perspective and can redirect my energy. When I laugh at myself or wax philosophical, I realize that my flaws are simply a part of being human and not a sign that I'm a crazy, pathetic, or a gluttonous person.

It also helps to share my vulnerabilities with others, talking about what's making me feel overwhelmed with someone I trust—a girlfriend, my mom, or my therapist. That's the best way to receive empathy. I am so fortunate to have people in my life who remind me of how I've shown empathy to others in similar situations. These reminders help me find my way back to steady ground so I can regain my composure and feel more competent and less self-critical.

Mindfully choosing empathy means seeking out the right people— people who care about you and your well-being. It takes noticing your actions and being nonjudgmental of your behavior and your feelings of shame, self-doubt, sadness, and anger. If I can notice when I'm judging myself, I can reach out for emotional support.

The next time you find yourself binging on junk food or mindlessly shopping, take a moment to give yourself the empathy you deserve. Remove your body from that tempting place (the kitchen or the store), find a new spot, and clear your mind. When you are safely away from the chips or shoes, pay attention to your feelings. Be kind and gentle with yourself. Recognize that your actions may have been mechanical and mindless, but give yourself credit for eventually noticing and putting a stop to them. All that's left is to begin again in the present moment.

Week 21

Finding Your Happy Place

I was introduced to the concept of *mindfulness of place* in my weekly meditation class. We were supposed to think of a place that brought about the particular feeling of *home*: comforting, safe, and in my case, a place filled with unbridled optimism. With all meditations, it's important to have an intention. With intention (or purpose), you have a place to focus your mind when it inevitably drifts. When you do something, *anything*, deliberately, you are fully present. Immediately, I focused on a vision of myself walking down Columbus Avenue on the Upper West Side of Manhattan on a beautiful fall day, wearing my denim jacket and boots, strolling past shops and restaurants, alone.

I don't know why that image popped into my mind. After all, I've never actually lived in Manhattan. True, I've spent countless hours walking along those streets, but I grew up in Israel and on Long Island. Nevertheless, every time I get the chance to go to New York City, I feel a sense of giddiness and anticipation that, to me, is the essence of joy.

I guess I'm a city girl at heart. Once I arrive, I'm filled with excitement and wonder, ready for the adventures to come. I love being in a place where the choices are endless, knowing that when I return, there will *still* be endless choices to consider. Manhattan satisfies my craving for grit, color, noise, culture, diversity, and surprises. When I am alone in NYC, I am off clock time, and I can linger in the experience as long as I want.

If you're looking for a respite during your crazy day and have only a few minutes, think about your version of home, a location that just feels *right*. It may be at the beach, a cabin in the mountains, a country road, or a park. It may even be in your own backyard. Wherever it is, try to focus on the place and your feelings about it—not of people or events that might have brought you there.

When I conjure up my favorite Columbus Avenue images, my heart beats a little faster. I recognize the urge to get on a plane or start planning my next trip. I try not to get too wrapped up in those details, and I focus on the feelings in my body and in my heart. I want to hold on to that contentment and never let go.

Often, we search for this elusive emotion, and when it comes, it disappears all too quickly without us recognizing it. We only miss contentment, it seems, once it's gone. So notice your contentment, including the sensations it produces in your body. Linger on all of it.

When I notice my own serenity and realize that I can bring it about deliberately between grocery shopping and work—or just before I drift off to sleep—that's an extraordinary feeling. All it takes is conjuring up a place that feels like home, wherever you happen to be.

Week 22

Lingering with Every Bite

When I say I love food, I mean I *love* food. You may relate to this statement or not, but either way, what I am about to tell you can help you appreciate your meals more deeply and with a whole new level of awareness.

From my childhood on, food has always felt like a celebration. On most evenings, my dad would arrive home by seven, fresh off the 5:40 train from New York City, and bound up the staircase from the garage, whistling. That was our cue to start the salad and set the table. Like Pavlov's dogs, we knew that dinner would be served as soon as my father walked into the kitchen, after he'd showered and changed into a freshly laundered shirt.

Unofficially, dinner always started before breakfast with a question from my mother: "What should I make tonight?" She didn't really expect feedback; she was mostly thinking out loud. After all, my mom was busy. She worked as a pediatric nurse and had to manage everything in our home with precision. Dinner was one of those things she managed. Whatever the meal—tuna casserole, meatloaf, a broiled chicken— she made it appear like magic, seemingly effortlessly. When she had more time, she would break out a recipe from her favorite Julia Child cookbook and wow us with a paella or whip up a Szechuan chicken dish she'd learned in her adult education cooking class. She always cooked with real, fresh food. There were no TV dinners and rarely food from a can (other than peas or fruit cocktail). We didn't have a microwave oven, and my mother thought that canned food was too salty. I grew up with the advantage of knowing exactly what I was eating.

Though my siblings and I rarely cooked a full meal (unless you count Campbell's tomato soup and a tuna fish sandwich) my mom's artful, relaxed way of putting food on the table made my sister and me curious about developing this skill for ourselves. Maybe that's why I tend to make a big thing out of dinner now that I have a family of my own. Besides the uninterrupted time it gives me to sit with the people I love, I enjoy the process of looking up a new recipe or perusing my favorite food blogs for something unique and tasty. I love to read the latest issue of *Bon Appetit* or browse *Epicurious.com* and drool over the beautiful images overflowing with color and texture.

You may hate the idea of preparing a meal. But if you like the way food tastes and appreciate a nice presentation, you can transform your next bite into a new and extraordinary experience. There are few daily rituals that include all of your senses, and savoring a meal is one of them. To mindfully eat a meal is to appreciate life itself.

Who has time for that? I'm not talking about spending more hours dicing and chopping and stirring. I'm talking about enjoying the time you have with each bite. If you're downing fare you've gotten from the drive-through, you can still notice, linger, taste the flavors and inhale the aromas. If you've made time to eat, then you have the time to savor and experience the moment.

Mindful eating is joyful eating! There are so many things to appreciate. Starting with a simple salad, you can look at each ingredient and feel gratitude for the sun and rain. You can relish the taste of a fresh tomato from your garden (or the farmer's market) and linger over the sweetness of a carrot or red bell pepper. If you're enjoying a plate of sushi, my favorite, you can feel the sticky rice on your tongue and the saltiness of the soy sauce bringing out each flavor. You can do this with grilled cheese and tomato soup or with a peanut butter and jelly sandwich. You can enjoy each and every morsel of a chicken drumstick or Greek yogurt with a drizzle of honey. If you want to raise the bar, break out that beautiful china and have a mindful eating celebration. To love food is to take the time to pay close attention to how it smells before it reaches your mouth—the subtle and powerful flavors, the textures, the silky smoothness, or a satisfying crunch.

Besides fueling your body, fully immersing yourself in the experience of eating feeds your soul. It can connect you to childhood memories or spur anticipation for a repeat performance. Stay with that awareness. Appreciate each bite as well as the remarkable feat it took to bring what you are eating to your plate. Nourish yourself.

Week 23

&

Pain, Pain Go Away!

It's a good bet that you probably devote a lot of your attention and focus to the feelings that consume you—whether it's anger after a fight with your boyfriend, exhaustion after a sleepless night, or simply being stressed. You talk to your girlfriends about an unfulfilling job or complain about your in-laws ad nauseam. You think that somehow the conversation will alleviate the pain or solve some problem.

Or maybe you have some physical ailment and your body needs relief. You apply all of your efforts into finding herbal remedies, making doctor's appointments, and filling prescriptions. Still, these maladies remain.

Mindfulness has taught me that when I place all of my attention on something, that thing comes to life—strong and determined. If your head hurts and you focus on it, the throbbing will just get worse. Instead, when you're in the throes of discomfort, try shifting your attention to the things in your life that are going fine, if only to alleviate some of your suffering.

In other words, use mindfulness and noticing to magnify the positive.

I'm not promising that once you focus on the positive, the negative things will go away. Rather, these painful feelings or thoughts can recede to the furthest part of your consciousness, allowing what *is* working in your life to become more evident.

This technique has been a lifesaver for me, partly because I have an immune system disorder that causes occasional inflammation in my hands. At times, these flare-ups can be so painful that they wake me in the middle of the night.

I was spending a lot of time treating this condition and worrying about it. I found a doctor who prescribed drugs, a nutritionist who recommended a gluten-free diet, and chat sites where I'd go to vent and learn. Yet the more attention I gave my malady, the more pain I experienced.

It came to a head one night when the pain got so bad that I just started crying. My husband didn't know what to do for me. He held my hand as I tried to calm myself. I began thinking of my breath, taking deep breaths, and focusing on the air passing through my lungs. My lungs were working just fine. I literally began to envision them expanding and contracting. *In and out. In and out.* My body relaxed, and exhaustion took over. Soon, I was off to sleep.

I noticed that the discomfort seemed to recede whenever I could get myself to relax, even if I was experiencing physical pain. By focusing on my breathing and noticing all the details and nuances of my breath— the air passing through my nostrils, the rise and fall of my belly—I could distract myself from the pain. I was focused on my breathing and not my physical discomfort.

To master this mindfulness technique, it's important to practice it when you're feeling just fine. It's like carrying a parachute; when you need it, you have it ready.

Try this now: Imagine any little ache or pain in your body. Maybe you're reading this book on a sofa or in bed. Maybe your shoulders are tight or your ankle is bothering you. Really pay attention to it. Notice how paying attention to it brings it to the forefront of your mind. Not something you welcome, right? Okay, now find another part of your body, something completely benign, maybe so much so that it feels invisible, like your fourth toe on your left foot. It's comfortable, or maybe there's a feeling of floating or air. Savor that, linger for a moment, and luxuriate in the pleasantness of it. Try to incorporate that sensation into your entire body. Feel it enveloping you. I'm guessing that your other pain has receded and that you're pretty relaxed.

You've just done a version of a formal technique to developing mindful awareness, called a body scan. In 1979, Jon Kabat-Zinn, a master of mindful meditation, introduced this practice at University of Massachusetts Medical School in his eight-week Mindfulness-Based Stress Reduction (MBSR) program for people with chronic pain. Since then, the technique has been successfully used in hospitals across the world to manage pain—and the benefits linger long after the eight-week training period.

If emotional pain is draining you and you're ruminating at night or complaining about it to someone who really likes drama, or if you're in physical pain of any kind, know that this mindful meditation practice can help you cope when you need it most. It may not solve all of your problems, but it *will* give you a respite from whatever ails you.

Week 24

=== ✑ ===

Intend to Do It and You Will

In late 1999, I suddenly had the desire to change my career—and I mean a complete and total change. I was finally ready to leave my marketing and media career to pursue my goal of becoming a marriage and family therapist. To do this, I'd have to attend graduate school, complete a three thousand-hour internship, and pass a set of state boards before opening my own private practice. It wouldn't be easy, but I felt as if I was following my passion.

By 2001, I was enrolled at California State University Northridge. I began learning and developing my skills, and I loved it.

I loved reading Viktor Frankl's *Man's Search for Meaning* and Irvin Yalom's *The Gift of Therapy,* I felt inspired to be the best I could be in my newly chosen profession. I attended workshops and met other aspiring therapists. That was the easy stuff. I didn't need to muster any motivation. I did it all without struggle because I was engaged in the process.

Then, in 2003, I got pregnant. After years of trying to have a baby, this was the *new* news in my life. I would devote my time and attention to bringing a little person into the world. The process derailed my efforts to become a therapist.

We all get derailed from time to time, often for legitimate reasons. The only way out is through fierce determination and unwavering focus—two things I had a hard time finding. When my son turned five, I *still* hadn't completed my required three thousand hours of counseling training. I began to get frustrated. I knew I had to get my internship hours in if I wanted to take my state exams and ultimately start practicing, but every time I'd come home from a day at the counseling center, I'd log my hours to find that I was still coming up short. It felt like I was running in circles, going to work, paying a sitter while I was working at an unpaid internship, moving forward only imperceptibly, if at all.

I voiced my concern to my meditation teacher during one of our Friday meetings. "I can't believe I haven't finished my hours," I said. "It's been so many years, and most of my peers are already done!" I felt embarrassed and ashamed that I couldn't do it.

"Well? What is your intention?" he asked.

Hmm. I hadn't thought of my intention for a long time. Intention is something you *want* to accomplish, like sitting still while meditating and concentrating on your breathing with the determination of returning to it when your mind wanders. Turns out I'd forgotten my intention. Instead, I was caught up in working, raising a little boy, tending to my marriage, and generally feeling tired and overwhelmed. I was in a daily automatic routine, stumbling toward my goal but rarely looking up to see if I was headed in the right direction or how far I still had to go. To complete my journey, I needed to make it a priority. I had to muster my energy and regain my focus and determination.

The first thing I did after that meditation class was have a heart-to-heart talk with my husband. If I was going to finish my internship hours, I needed his support in the form of his pitching in more at home and picking our son up from school or preparing dinner so that I could devote the necessary time to reach my goal. I feel very fortunate that my husband encouraged me wholeheartedly because it wasn't easy. We all needed to make adjustments so that I could realize my dream. My husband kept his word, and I sharpened my focus. I completed my hours and studied for my boards, and was licensed within six months.

Whatever your intention, you need to decide that it's truly worth it and that you're willing to make the accommodations and sacrifices to accomplish your goal. If it's a financial goal, then vacation, nights on the town, and takeout four times a week may have to wait. If it's a health goal, like losing weight, you will likely have to curb your calorie intake and step it up at the gym. Most important, you must approach your goal with fierce determination and resolve—with an intention to make your dreams a reality. Having support from your spouse and your girlfriends is icing on the cake.

And, if you get diverted, as we often do, remind yourself of your intention, be kind, and begin again.

Week 25

Rest **Is Not a Dirty Word**

With all this work you've been doing to improve your life by noticing and staying focused and present, you may feel uncertain about whether you can actually *do* this thing called mindfulness, let alone stick with it for longer than it takes to read this book.

That's when it's good to remember that mindfulness doesn't have to feel like a job. It is something that you can develop over time, organically, as you gently start to notice yourself being present. If you get tired or feel overwhelmed, it's also key to notice when you require rest and relaxation. Everything starts with noticing, followed by intention.

On any given day, I can check in and know if I'm in a moving-forward mode with the energy and determination to proceed or if I need to rest. When I say rest, I mean that I need to give my mind (and sometimes my body) a break from planning, doing, achieving, setting goals, meeting deadlines, or crossing another item off of my ever-present to-do list. I know I need rest when I lose focus, get distracted (or, in my case, more easily distracted than usual), feel overwhelmed, or become exceedingly impatient. I'll also notice that I'm physically tired, forgetful, and generally done. When I get to the point where I realize I've been running on empty, it's time to get off the hamster wheel.

Whether I'm deliberately paying attention to my need for rest or am jarred into noticing it, that's when I begin the process of intention.

Setting an intention to rest may sound ridiculous. But when you don't, it's easy to get lost in a trance of mindless online surfing or hours of sitting in front of the television when what's required is an hour spent daydreaming or reading a good book.

Your intention for R & R may need some planning and support. You may crave a spa day to remove yourself from your daily chores or commitments. You may want to schedule a few hours on the couch at home. When I set my intention on deliberately creating the space and time to rest, I take a book into my backyard and read until I'm feeling satisfied that I've gotten the break I crave. Sometimes, I'm satisfied after twenty minutes. If I need more of a hiatus, I like to relax at a café and people watch without a book or iPhone to distract me. I simply enjoy not having to engage in any banter or deal with other responsibilities. Doing nothing—or very little—feels like a luxury worth indulging in.

Week 26

&

The Easiest Cure for Insomnia—Ever

How many nights have you endured hours in bed, waiting and waiting for your mind to stop racing so you can relax and get some sleep?

Until just a short time ago, this was a common occurrence in my life. There could be a hundred reasons for my wakefulness: too much wine or chocolate, crazy hormones, a book I couldn't put down, or my cat jumping on my head. Insomnia caused by worry and rumination was most common—and most annoying.

Not anymore. Now, when I'm in that wired, wide-awake state of mind, I remind myself to go to my nonthinking place, and bam! In no time, I'm out.

Getting to a nonthinking place may sound impossible, but with some practice, it's possible to intentionally notice or observe your thoughts rather than getting caught up in the story of them. When you're caught up in your story, you are *thinking* instead of observing. Thinking isn't great for sleep because it usually means you're trying to figure out what should happen next. You may be working to solve some critical problem, a conversation you had with your mother, what to serve at your next dinner party, or what color to paint the bathroom. All of these thoughts can be going on in your mind at once, which isn't conducive to a good night's rest.

To remove yourself from these kind of ruminative, obsessive thoughts, you must intentionally *watch* them. Then, once you're observing all that inner flitting around, the next step is to intentionally recognize that while your mind may be trying to figure stuff out, you are not required to participate in any of it. It's a difficult concept to grasp, and sometimes it's difficult to achieve. But with practice, you can do it.

The important thing is remembering that watching, observing, and noticing your thoughts is not the same as thinking. When you are simply recognizing that your thoughts exist, you're not engaging in them or trying to solve anything. When you observe rather than think, you remove the burden of anxiety, allowing your body and mind to stay present and relax. The process is akin to formal meditation, which involves simply noticing your thoughts, letting them go, and then returning to your anchor, whether that's your breathing, ambient sounds in the room, or physical sensations like your heartbeat.

To get a sense of what this noticing feels like, take a moment to look at something in your immediate environment. In my kitchen, at this moment, I notice a dirty dish in the sink. I look at it and notice its color, the ridges on the rim, and the bumps and clumps of food left behind. That's noticing. If I remember that I asked my son to put his dish in the dishwasher or that the recipe for the meal I just ate was a bit disappointing or that I have to buy more dish detergent, I'm no longer present. I'm no longer noticing the dish that is in front of me. Instead, I'm thinking.

To practice *noticing*, I invite you to bring your attention, right now, to something and look at it with sustained attention. Notice when your mind drifts, then bring your attention back to the object without judgment. If you practice this when you're awake, you'll have an easier time doing it when you have insomnia... The more often you try this practice of mindful awareness, the easier it will be to recognize the difference between observing and thinking—and to treat yourself to a restful sleep without the aid of Ambien.

Week 27

A Friend in Need

You are listening to someone's dreadful news. Suffering is occurring. Your close girlfriend's dog died, or your coworker's husband was in a car accident.

Most of us feel uncomfortable or even burdened by bad news. Understandably, someone else's bad news may have us imagining bad things happening to our own loved ones. It may remind us of our losses and our mortality.

When you hear bad news, you may feel the urge to jump in and help solve some problem. Your anxiety and fear may have you asking questions that your friend can't answer or doesn't want to answer. That's frustrating for both of you.

Resist that urge to fix. The best thing to do is to simply *be* there. Listen, hold her hand, and be present. Your role as a friend and confidante, in and of itself, is precious. That means staying calm and reflective when someone you care about is overwhelmed with sadness or fear. Your calmness will bring clarity, and your reflection will keep you from internalizing the other person's pain. Staying impartial and nonjudgmental is also crucial for helping you and your friend accept whatever has happened, so she can begin to heal. Chatter, advice, and busy movement take attention away from the moment. And this moment requires you to be there, calmly.

This advice may seem strange. Perhaps you believe that rushing onto the scene and recounting the details of a tragedy give you some sort of control over the situation and will bring you some peace. And maybe, for a moment, offering a brownie or making a cup of tea will provide some relief. Soon though, after the effects of the sugar wear off, the rawness of the situation will return.

It's not easy to witness a loved one in pain, but by staying aware of your intention, which is to ease your friend's suffering, you'll be able to quietly sit next to her, which is the first step to helping someone heal.

Week 28
&
No Judgments, Please!

A very important part of becoming mindful is noticing judgments—your own self-critical voice ("I hate my thighs!") or the one you project onto others ("I can't believe she just did that!")

Our culture only feeds the frenzy. We are bombarded by snarky tabloids (*Who Wore it Best?*) and derisive comments on social media, all of which contribute to a hater mentality. Unless you notice your own contribution to this rhetoric, you'll continue with those mean judgments and forget what you *truly* want: to be heard, understood, and accepted for your own ideas and points of view, without any judgments.

It's tough to do that because we all have opinions about almost everything. That's not a bad thing ... *unless* you can't differentiate between your personal preferences and a judgment. It's the difference between saying, "That pair of jeans makes you look fat," and "I prefer the boot cut; it somehow makes you look taller." The difference is simple: criticism versus preference. The latter is so much nicer. Like when you're sharing burritos with your bestie and you say, "Mexican food is usually too spicy for me," rather than, "I hate Mexican food!" Changing your language allows the other person to see things from your point of view, understand you, and even empathize.

Before beginning my own mindful meditation practice, I never thought much about my own judgments. I'd notice when others were judging me, when I felt criticized, or when someone expressed disappointment in me, but it was only when my meditation practice started to take hold that I began noticing my own judgments and how frequently they surfaced in my daily life. I noticed that I said things like, "That was a horrible movie," instead of, "I prefer romantic comedies," or "*That's* what you're wearing?"—accompanied by an eye roll—when my husband showed up ready for a date night in a sweater from 1999. In each circumstance, I could have opted to make my point without criticism. Date night would have gotten off to a better start if I'd said, "When you wear your blue sweater, your eyes really light up."

To be clear, what you believe to be right or wrong, good or bad, is simply your opinion. How you communicate your opinion is the difference between sounding judge-y or not. Noticing your words when you state a preference or deliver a critique can make all the difference in your relationships. If your words and attitude imply that your values are better or right, then you've moved into the territory of judgment. Are you, in fact, smarter, superior, or *better*?

No one likes to be judged. When you judge others, you inevitably leave them feeling alienated, misunderstood, and angry. Once you start decreeing that your opinion is more important or correct than anyone else's, you can easily fall into the trap of believing that your opinion *is* fact, especially in situations where you are passionately expressing your beliefs when you really want to be heard and understood. This can happen even when you're discussing something as frivolous as the latest TV series or more tricky topics like politics.

Recently, I got into a heated discussion over the latter. I happened to be on the side of a female candidate, and the other person was on the side of anyone else but her. I was determined to explain to this person why I believed she was the best candidate for the job. I was open to answering questions about my beliefs and the reasons for my preference. What astonished me was that this person had no questions—only opinions (mostly negative) of my preferred candidate. It didn't matter what I had to say. She wanted me to agree with her simply because she'd uttered her personal opinion. She learned little from me because there was no curiosity on her part, and I learned little from her because she didn't offer any rationale for her choices.

You've probably heard the saying that you should never bring up politics or religion in good company. Well, to believe that is to keep your thoughts and opinions to yourself, lest you be judged. It's easy to feel a bit exposed when these topics come up because of uncertainty over how others may perceive us. Most of us don't have enough practice at mindfully presenting our opinions, especially when it comes to these hot topics.

It's possible to dive into these difficult conversations and not judge or feel judged. The first step is awareness. Notice the language you use, which can help you fine-tune the way you express your beliefs. That means speaking clearly with words that describe your preferences as well as acknowledging that you are talking about your preferences based on what you've learned. If my friend had acknowledged my point of view and offered a hint at her candidate's accomplishments and values, I would have had an opportunity to weigh the candidate's credentials and maybe even change my opinion. At the very least, I would have walked away understanding her more instead of feeling annoyed and shut down.

The second step to having a difficult conversation without judgment is to stay open and curious. That means resisting the temptation to defend yourself when you hear a critical tone of voice. Instead, ask open-ended questions to clarify the other person's point of view. (Really? Tell me more about that. That's interesting. I didn't know you felt this way. Why is that?) If you're uncomfortable asking questions, you can always reflect and repeat what the other person said to clarify their position. To do it, say something like, "Let me understand you. What you're describing is …" Then give them the opportunity to further discuss or clarify.

It's not as difficult as you might imagine. Just pause, notice, and listen. Notice your urge to interrupt or negate the other's thoughts. Ask for further explanation with interest and kindness. You never know what you may learn from someone's passionate beliefs. You don't have to agree. You just have to take them in. After all, it's human nature to want to feel understood. By being deliberate and conscious in your choice of language, and by expressing preferences instead of judgments, you allow others to understand and accept you for who you really are—and you can do the same.

Week 29

Put. The. Phone. Down.

The essence of mindfulness is being fully present in your experience. For me, that state of being happens most fully when I attend a live concert. Watching a live performance, to me, is the ultimate mindful sensory experience. I get to enjoy a show by an artist I love, singing and dancing along to my favorite tunes while hanging out with my husband (who does this sort of *being* really well) or my girlfriends.

Recently, I caught a Maroon 5 concert at the Los Angeles Forum. I endured horrific traffic and nightmare parking scenarios so that I could get up front and personal with one of my favorite bands. To truly savor the experience, I have a tried-and-true pre-concert ritual: I do a little sing-along and video binge beforehand, followed by an internet search for the latest online blogs and news about the current tour. Some might think it a bit excessive, but it puts me in the right mood.

When I arrived at the venue, totally pumped and prepped, I discovered that though I had paid a premium for floor seats, I still wouldn't be able to see much. (I'm just over five feet tall, and I wasn't in the first twenty rows.) Instead, I had to look at the video monitors above my head to watch Adam Levine come alive. I felt disconnected.

Adam told us how much he appreciated all of us for being willing to crane our necks, view the monitors, and use binoculars (for the nosebleed section). He also commented on what he saw in front of him: the incessant use of phones in front of faces taking photos and videos.

He told us that the phones also made him feel a bit disconnected—from the audience.

He asked us all to put down our phones and video recorders and *feel* the music, to listen and watch. He wanted everyone's devoted attention. He felt the distance and was trying to bridge the gap.

What a difference it made! I immediately felt the mood in the air shift. Instead of phones being held high, to better capture the show, we were swaying to the music and belting out the songs. I could see Adam on that stage, *looking* directly at people. He didn't have to fight the cameras for attention. He simply felt everyone's presence. We were with him.

Perhaps you're using your phone to capture the mood of your night out or the food you're about to consume. Maybe you're on vacation and feel that you have to capture a breathtaking sunset. It's natural to want evidence of your experiences to feed your memories later on, but there comes a point when phones and cameras rob us of the joy of the moment.

Before you pull out your smartphone and start clicking away, ask yourself a few questions: Will taking a photo now give me a more complete experience than the one I'm already having? Will I be reliving this moment when I glance at the photos in a month? If not, why distract yourself? Instead, pause, look around, and immerse yourself in the moment. You'll experience the kind of joy you won't need a photograph to recall.

Week 30

The Future Is Now

One of my favorite words in the English language is *anticipation*. It conjures up the excited feeling of wonderful things to come with a shiver of giddiness and hope on the horizon.

Is it possible to truly be in the present moment if you're anticipating something in the future? That's tricky.

Mindfulness is about noticing; it's about being aware of each one of your senses at any given moment. If I'm feeling love or warmth toward someone I am with, I can notice that easily and take it in. But if I've planned a trip with my family and the day is drawing near, is the excitement I feel an example of mindfulness? After all, I'm thinking about the future, not the current moment. This kind of delicious anticipation is absolutely mindful because you're connected to the physical and emotional experience of the moment. And it's not the same thing as getting caught up in the logistics of an event or planning.

If you want to understand mindfulness, it's critical to understand the difference between *thinking* and *feeling*. Take the vacation example: Anticipating an exciting new experience almost always begins with thinking, planning, and paying thoughtful attention to the details of your getaway. Once these details, like location, budget, etc., are finalized, the anticipation sets in. It's a separate phase from the planning and the event itself. It's like a bracket of time where you get to relish the excitement of what's to come.

When I'm lost in anticipation, I physically feel joy. I can linger in that feeling and be present with my happiness. Anticipating something wonderful in the future can help harness the emotion of happiness, notice it, and appreciate it when it's present. Best of all, it's possible to stay with this exquisite feeling and linger in it as long as you notice it.

We are all looking for the feeling of pure happiness. Often, we believe that it should be present all the time, and we're disappointed when it's not. We worry that something is wrong, or why we haven't found it, but feelings are transient. They come and go.

Once you notice yourself feeling joy about an upcoming trip or whatever you're anticipating, it's so important to savor it and let yourself luxuriate in it. That's the best way to cultivate more of it.

Week 31

Whine Or Wine?

When you're stressed or bored or you've just gotten home from a two-hour commute, do you find yourself automatically reaching for a glass of Pinot? Or maybe it's a cookie or Xanax? We often use these seductive substances to find fast relief. I'm not here to judge, but if you're not careful, it can be easy to spiral into rationalization and even addiction.

As for my own cravings, I *need* a three o'clock hit of caffeine to keep me going for the rest of the afternoon, after-school pickup, and dinner prep. I'll pull into Starbucks and reload my card with another twenty dollars to get me through the month while thinking, *I've got to stop doing this!* Whether your poison of choice is caffeine or cannabis (easier than ever to get here in LA) it's important to notice what mood you're trying to ameliorate. Are you bored? Tired? Anxious? Something else?

An antidote to some of these cravings is to train your focus on something other than what you are craving. It won't always feel easy, which I know from all the times I've refilled my Starbucks card. It takes intention, practice, and patience.

For me, a turning point came when I began working with kids who have attention issues. Whenever they'd get distracted from our conversation or game, I'd prompt them to immediately shift their attention and hold onto one of my favorite tools—my Huggtopus, a plush toy with eight arms, squishy body, and an open mouth sized just right for "emotion balls," which Huggie can swallow (each one is marked with an emotion like *afraid, angry,* or *sad*). I tell the child to hold Huggtopus tightly, select the emotion ball that reflects what he or she is feeling, and put it into Huggie's mouth. The angry ball was the most common choice by far. Together, we'd talk about the anger, which often led to the kids revealing that they were frustrated with themselves. Whatever the cause of their frustration, the game made it easier for them to focus on exactly what they were feeling and notice their mood. When you notice something like a mood or an urge, you are more capable of making conscious choices. Often, these kids would choose to come back to the conversation or game and complete the task at hand.

When I saw how well the technique worked in my office, I suggested that parents try it at home when their kids were struggling to concentrate on homework. As a stand-in for Mr. Huggie, I suggested using another enticing object, like a cute eraser, a little car, or a Lego piece. They wouldn't necessarily have to name the emotion, but their ability to sustain their attention on the toy helped get them to a still place. The parents often reported that the more frequently the kids practiced taking a break and focusing on staying still, the better they were able to refocus and complete their work for the next day.

Some parents liked the technique so much that they began using it to curb their own urges. Some would put a sticky note with "What do you *really* want?" on the medicine cabinet to deter them from giving in to a go-to Ambien each night. I sometimes put an apple on top of my coffee maker as reminder that I didn't need more than one cup of java to get me going. These anchors make it easier to stop in your tracks— in the middle of an urge—so you can notice your feelings, name your cravings, and consciously make different choices.

If you have regular cravings that you're trying to curb, select an object and focus on it to get in touch with what's going on for you emotionally. Are you hoping that a glass of wine (or two) will distract you from feelings of loneliness? Try buying yourself a pretty bouquet and placing it next to your liquor cabinet or wine rack. Flowers can have a positive effect on your mood. Smelling a rose or even a bunch of rosemary can shift your state of mind. Placing a fresh sprig of rosemary from my garden on the dashboard before picking up my son from school has helped deter me from a Starbucks run en route.

It's not easy to make these different choices when we're responding on auto-pilot to our urges. To make it easier, create an alternate physical stimuli that can divert your attention so the next time that need surfaces, you're prepared to respond differently.

Week 32

Calling All BFFs!

If you're ready to tackle a dream, how can you succeed? What will that journey look like?

One great lesson I learned long ago is to look around at the multitude of talent that surrounds me (girlfriends, relatives, mentors, and peers) and note their special aptitudes. I do this when I'm introduced to new people. I notice their ability to listen or their sage comments during conversation. I notice patience and fearlessness among my friends. I notice and admire a particular capacity for support and encouragement, and I notice a flair for a certain passion in life (say with painting or fashion). This kind of noticing helps me remember who to turn to when I'm reaching toward my own goals and aspirations. With the added support of my people—from friends who are great at saving and investing money to the cousin who always knows the best new restaurant to check out—I've discovered that I can realize more than I might have imagined.

Sometimes I can be that friend for someone else. I have a girlfriend I'd always thought of as the consummate Francophile. We talked about Paris so much—the art, the cafes, the Seine—that I assumed she had been there countless times. One day, she mentioned that she'd never actually been to Paris! I was shocked. When I probed a bit further, I discovered that she'd never had a plan for traveling there (she wasn't deliberate about achieving her dream). She did, however, have a desire (intention).

It can be tough to tell the difference between having an intention and being deliberate and being determined. To clarify, having an intention means that you desire some type of result. Maybe your intention is to stay focused, learn Japanese, become a teacher, or simply listen to your breathing right now.

Being determined, on the other hand, means that you've set your intention and have made a commitment to achieving that intention. You'll need determination to keep moving forward, which is fueled by your attitude and the priorities you set.

Got it? When you're being deliberate, you've set an intention and you're determined. You need to plan and focus on staying committed. This is usually where most of us get sidetracked, stuck, or disillusioned. If you know what's getting in your way, it's easier to keep going—and it's even easier if you have support.

My friend needed that support. I wanted to help her figure out what was getting in the way of her achieving her dream since she certainly had the time and the means to get on a plane and take a week to indulge her fantasy. What was holding her back? After talking, I discovered that there were a few perceived obstacles in her way. First, she didn't have a passport (easy application process). Next, she said she was always too busy with work (though she had accrued more than enough vacation time). I didn't buy it. Something was blocking her. I offered to help move her through this block, which was very exciting for me since I love to travel and enjoy the planning process.

One afternoon, as we sat poolside during a weekend getaway with the Sunday *New York Times* travel section, we began the process of planning the trip of her life. At first, I asked her about the experience she wanted to have. That was easy since she'd dreamed of going to Paris for years. She knew she wanted to stay in a hotel near an iconic Parisian landmark. The harder part was the commitment. I asked, "Are you really going to do this?" She told me that she was.

Next, she needed a plan and to stay focused on that plan, which included a pre-trip to-do list: get the time off from work, book the hotel, and buy the plane tickets. For some reason, the little obstacle of the passport kept getting in her way. I offered to help her fill out the application, go the to post office for the little photos, and walk her through each step. All she would have to do was hand over the fee so that she could proceed to Paris. She finally boarded an Air France flight from Los Angeles in pursuit of her vision.

How many times have you had a dream or commitment where you believe you're all in—only to find that time keeps passing without you achieving your goals? If you look closely, you may find that your plan needs some fine-tuning or that you need to break it down into smaller steps that feel less overwhelming. This is where the support of a friend and her talent can be essential. Everyone needs a cheerleader.

Week 33

❧

What I Learned on My Family Vacation

I'm the designated "arranger of things" in my family. That includes after-school activities, carpools, dental appointments, dinner parties, and date nights. I guess it's no surprise that I take on arrangements for our annual family getaway. I always begin the vacation-planning phase with some desire of my own—or I used to. I would fantasize about Europe (with friends), a weekend getaway somewhere romantic (with my husband), or an adventure with my family. Whatever it was, I'd begin by figuring out where *I* wanted to go and what *I* wanted to get out of the experience.

The problem was that there is no *I* in *we*. I learned this the hard way when, a few years ago, my husband and I returned from a vacation with friends who were celebrating a big anniversary. There were lots of laughs, beautiful sightseeing, great food, and fantastic company. It was the trip I was hoping for, and that's what I got. I also got the silent treatment from my husband when we returned home. As the planner, I failed to listen when he told me that he really wanted to check out the vineyards (and maybe have a day or two alone together). He'd mentioned those things but I may have forgotten to consider his needs in the midst of my planning. The result was regret and resentment, and I felt terrible about that. I was determined to do things differently the next time.

It came down to my failure to honor the *other* person. We do this when we ask, listen, and pay attention to the other person's suggestions and dreams—even if they seem outrageous. When your partner isn't feeling seen, heard, or truly noticed, it can really throw a wrench into your relationship—not to mention your vacation.

Week 34

Being the Calm in the Eye of the Storm

With my formal meditation practice, my ability to notice, stay focused, and be still has helped me tune in to whatever I happen to be doing. I can do this even when there is chaos around me—blaring music or background dialogue from the TV, the sound of my husband on the phone in the next room, my son running in and out of the kitchen (where I'm trying to write this chapter), or my cat constantly trying to jump onto my lap. This is how my house operates on any given day. I sit here, aware of the activity, yet I am able to write sentences on this page. This form of attention is called *co-awareness*. It is a state of being aware of everything around you, as you remain especially focused on one thing.

The key to achieving co-awareness is to stay committed to your anchor or intention. You may notice the background activity, but you choose to move those distractions to the far reaches of your mind, recognizing that they exist but not engaging in them. I intend to finish writing this chapter and continue to be mindful of the words I am forming while noticing my son opening the refrigerator. I may get pulled in for a short time—"Wait until dinner!"—but with dedication, I bring my attention back to the job at hand.

It's easy to use the distractions of life as an excuse for not getting stuff done. We are constantly beckoned by requests from others, interrupted by a cacophony of sounds, and bombarded by our own stray thoughts. Sometimes, we are even cajoled, coaxed, guilted, and lured by others into getting *their* stuff done. Often we are convinced that those other things or other people should take precedence over our own commitments.

By noticing this tendency toward distraction and paying attention to how and when your attention goes astray, you can start to practice co-awareness. This can done while in a formal meditation, too. Notice your mind's busyness as soon as you close your eyes. There's no time – or need - to get ready because there will always be something going on in your mind. With sheer determination and intention, you bring your attention back to your breathing. Your attention will drift a thousand times, but each time you notice it, you recommit to your intention, which is to focus on your breath even while your mind is busy thinking other thoughts.

The same principle applies to any moment in your daily life when you must pay attention to one thing while other distracting stuff is going on. You must deliberately bring your focus to that one thing with an intention of staying attuned to the task at hand.

That's co-awareness, and I encourage you to practice it during your day. You can do it at your office (while others are conversing around you). You can do it while cooking dinner (as your child plays loud music in his room). You can do it at the movie theater (while the kids in front of you chat on their cell phones). You can even do it when you're hanging out with your friends (while your phone buzzes at the dinner table.)

When you remain focused in the midst of chaos, you only have one thing to do: strive to be fully present, again and again.

Week 35

&

Aging in Real Time

One day, you wake up and wonder how it happened so fast. You get out of bed and look at yourself in the mirror. Lo and behold, it's right there—a few more lines, a little extra flesh around the middle. I know because it happened to me. Just yesterday, it seems, I was somehow more vivid, more alive, and more relevant.

It's not always easy to accept yourself as you move further away from your fresh-faced, taut-bodied twenties. Often, the fact that you are no longer the youngest person in the room can hit like a ton of bricks. I was in my mid-forties when I began to notice signs of my own aging. Before then, it had barely crossed my mind that one day I would be like the nice older ladies who'd surrounded me as a kid in New York (in a nice Jewish family), talking about their aches and pains and cholesterol levels and doctors appointments. I, now, live in the land of the "beautiful people," and the conversations focus on facelifts, kale, and the various vitamins and potions that would supposedly slow the aging process. I decided I was going to join that team. I knew I couldn't prevent aging altogether, but I was going to delay it for as long as possible.

I succumbed to the promises of green tea, ginkgo biloba, and, ultimately, Botox. At first, I was a bit skeptical about getting injected with needles filled with some mysterious concoction that promised to take away my laugh lines. But I discovered that, in five minutes, I could be in and out of my appointment, looking and feeling five years younger. I'm not saying that this is what you should do, but those were the first steps in my mind. I was determined to look and feel fabulous and battle all the physical signs in the mirror (and on my body). In other words, I was in denial about the magnitude of what was happening. After all, I was in relatively good health and had been at least somewhat active my whole life. I was going to be okay.

Then I turned fifty.

I'd prepared myself for that milestone for several months, but something magical happened—something I hadn't been expecting. I started noticing that I was *different* from the younger generation, but not *worse*. This transformation took place over time and at specific moments. Once, during yoga class, I noticed all these beautiful women around me, women who were mostly my age. I realized that I was in awe of them. They seemed content and exuded strength. Weren't these women better role models than the seemingly younger Photoshopped women on magazine covers?

Another time, during a swim at the pool club, I noticed a woman in the lap lane next to me. She was quite graceful and strong, in her sixties, swimming and moving rhythmically, practically gliding. And on New Year's Eve, surrounded by my friends, I realized we looked fabulous all dolled up; confident and glowing.

That's when I started to consciously appreciate the body I had. When I could do that, I was able to accept that it was my responsibility to take active steps to keep myself healthy and strong by hiking more, eating less red meat, doing more yoga, and consuming less sugar. Just as important, I needed to do more looking inward and less looking outward. I had to focus more on now and less on then.

Comparing my body to the woman I was ten or twenty years earlier did not serve me. It only increased my suffering. Because of my meditation practice, I realized that I had some control over that kind of suffering. I had to experience myself in a new, fresh way. I had to adopt beginner's mind for the older person I now was. I wanted to feel at peace with my body and my face, lines and all, and celebrate the life I was living. I knew that meant bringing my focus and attention to my blessings and being grateful for them. Once I could do that, I had the power to expand the positive experiences in my life and shrink the negative. I could take responsibility for my aging self rather than denying it. I could simply do the best I could with what I had (yes, that still included getting Botox).

In short, I needed to live more mindfully and be more discerning about what I ate, how I slept, and how I used the mirror—as a reflection of my state of mind rather than merely a refection of my skin.

You've probably done some denying too. You've probably been hard on yourself, especially when you notice a new gray hair or wrinkle. I implore you to see grace and loveliness the next time you look in the mirror. Better yet, walk away from the mirror—especially the magnifying kind—and look around at your family and friends and the good stuff you've created. If you find that you're in a place of acceptance, then create new goals that celebrate your intellect, wisdom, and love. When you arrive at a new chapter of your life, embrace it. You don't need Botox for that.

Week 36

~ ❦ ~

Road Rage and Other
Life Annoyances

The next time someone cuts you off on the highway, slips into the express line at the grocery store with an *extra* item (or three), or rushes in late to a meeting, distracted and discombobulated, think about your reaction. Is it hospitable or annoyed?

You might think that hospitality means inviting your in-laws for a visit, letting a friend of a friend crash on your couch, or even hosting an afternoon tea party. That's not it. In the realm of mindfulness, hospitality has everything to do with attitude and extending yourself in a way that is gracious, kind, and compassionate.

Showing hospitality is a way of embracing others and extending kindness. On the road, in the market, or in the office, I can be deliberate and remind myself that I have a choice to see others with compassion. I can let the hurried driver pass without flipping him the bird. I can let the shopper load the conveyor with her extra items and even say a polite good morning. I can allow a harried co-worker a nod or smile to let her know that it's all okay. I can choose not to add any more distress to a person's already-stressed-out day.

The idea of extending hospitality may sound like simply letting go of the small stuff, but I think it's more than that. Being hospitable is making a conscious and deliberate effort to recognize and notice the other person *and* your own reactions and judgments. I practice hospitality during my weekly meditation class when someone enters the room during our discussion or silent sitting meditation. I stop myself from getting grouchy by deliberately focusing on the sounds around me rather than getting caught up in any negative thoughts. I can smile and be happy that the latecomer was able to join—despite whatever prevented them from being punctual.

There are times you may feel entitled to lash out if someone cuts you off on the road, especially if you've had a difficult day. However, there's a real cost to letting your everyday interactions be defined by irritation, frustration, and negativity. You'll feel terrible, and you'll make everyone else feel terrible too.

Think about how you feel when *you're* on the receiving end of inhospitable behavior. When someone gives you the evil eye because of some slight (or grand) error in your actions, it doesn't feel good. What if you took a moment to curb that initial, grouchy reaction and approached other people's errors with less anger and more generosity?

The trick to getting a grip on your attitude is to notice yourself and your immediate reactions. It's a process that starts at the beginning of your day, noticing your mood and attitude before you step out of the door, noticing the effort it takes to smile at your child or spouse while getting ready for work. When you are aware of your own *willingness* to have more patience even if you don't quite feel it, you're more likely to carry that patient attitude with you for a bit.

On the other hand, if you find that you're doing a lot of eye rolling, take a moment to breathe. If you can, ask yourself if it might be possible to shift your attitude to a more neutral position. While you can't magically flip a switch and make yourself happy, you can turn down the intensity. You can take a step back and assess your own state of mind without further exacerbating your foul mood.

When you consciously choose kindness and hospitality, you'll make everyone else's day better, transform your mood from impatience to calmness, and have a better day yourself.

Week 37

Hurry Up and Wait

Waiting is not one of my strong suits. I have trouble cooling my heels before an appointment with my doctor. I have a really hard time waiting for friends to arrive at my house for a dinner party when the appetizers are getting cold. I am definitely irked when a client is late and then wants to stay an extra fifteen minutes to make up for lost time (and money.) Why is this time thing a *thing*?

Maybe it's the impatient New Yorker in me or the way my parents drilled the importance of punctuality into me from an early age. Maybe it's that I live in a mostly unpunctual world, especially now with cell phones. People feel exonerated once they text: *Running late! B there soon!* When I am the one waiting, I start to get anxious. *What if I got the time wrong?* I check and recheck my calendar, and then I just get angry. I may look calm on the outside, but I'm roiling inside.

Am I venting here? A little. Blame the doctor's appointment yesterday where I waited for more than an hour, my son fidgeting impatiently and exposed to G-d knows what germs, to get a simple test done. Not fair!

Time is money, sure, but that's not what bothers me. How about respect or lost opportunities? Thinking about all of these things can get me into a real state, but I try to be mindful instead of throwing a temper tantrum. At the doctor's office, I deliberately began doing some deep breathing to alleviate some anxiety and blow off some steam. I took a deep breath through my nose and counted to six as I released it, feeling my lungs expanding and feeling my abdomen as I collected myself. I noticed the air in my nostrils, and I concentrated on counting and breathing simultaneously. It's something I learned in yoga class, something I now practice often in my everyday life. Deep breathing, a sensory experience, brings immediate calm and stillness, and being calm and still has a huge affect on my mood.

If someone is *really* late, I try not to think the worst (*I hope they didn't get into a car accident!*) and make an effort to be still. When I notice that I'm about to lose it, I know I can return to being quiet. If that doesn't work, I will start an activity to take my mind off my impatience. I concentrate on organizing my shoes or cleaning the bathroom. At least I'm being productive.

I find that doing something deliberate that requires my attention and focus is an incredibly helpful way to stop ruminating or obsessing when I'm anxious and need a distraction to keep me from going over the edge.

If you are the one who's nearly always late (for an appointment, a date, or for work) I could suggest many helpful tools (a watch or Smartphone, for instance). The first step is to honestly look at your pattern and take a more mindful approach to managing your time. You can analyze your tendency to be late, ask yourself why. You can berate yourself for letting someone down or begin a deliberate accounting of your time by noticing any recurring patterns. Do you run late to work or when you're meeting up with a friend? Are you late for appointments—or is there just a general ten-minute delay with everything? All of these delays, big and small, matter. The consequence is the same: loss of respect or even trust.

When it comes to my time—or anyone's time—it's important to acknowledge its value and be aware of what it means to others. Forgive me for coming down hard on this issue. I know I sound inflexible, but when you stay aware of the time and make an effort to be punctual, you are engaged in an awareness of your responsibility to yourself and to others. You are putting yourself in another person's shoes because you are thinking about how being late or being kept waiting affects everyone involved. You are showing empathy and recognizing that these things can affect the quality of your relationships.

Sometimes stuff just happens, including unexpected delays, but developing a habit of minding the clock can be a way of showing others that you really are someone who cares.

Week 38

&

Removing Yourself from the Driver's Seat

Here's an ugly truth: I think I'm a better driver than my husband. That doesn't always bode well for our marriage. As arguments go, the driving fight (who's going to drive and who is going to try to keep their mouth shut while the other is driving) is the one that's most likely to happen between us. Neither wants the other to drive. I would rather have control over my Sirius stations and the AC level than sit in the passenger seat, trying to ignore the red brake lights of the cars in front of us (as I hold the dashboard, silently cursing.)

We both have been driving for over thirty years, but when he is behind the wheel, I can't seem to stop myself from telling him where to go or commenting on his speed, whether too fast or too slow. Either I'm not-so-subtly bracing myself against the dashboard on the off chance that it will keep me from flying out the window if we crash or I'm using air brakes while clutching the door handle. If I think he's driving too slowly, I suggest that the next lane is wide open, *honey*.

It's not surprising that we end up raising our voices, is it? Just thinking about it brings to mind the important issue of trust—or the lack of it. I clearly have trouble *trusting* that my husband will get us wherever we are going in one piece (though I have no reason not to). If you have trouble with trust, get ready to tackle the issue head-on.

Trusting is scary and for good reason. Putting yourself in someone else's hands is not a decision to take lightly. You wouldn't trust just anyone to shuttle you around in a car if you didn't believe they possessed the skill to get you there safely (Uber notwithstanding). Once you're buckled in and have decided to give over that trust, you need to know when to keep your comments to yourself, especially if that person is your spouse.

How do you quell the urge to flinch or call out instructions? How do you just let go and trust? Trust is a decision, and decisions are often based on logic. If the person you are with has proven to be trustworthy and dependable in the past, you can be reasonably confident that they'll continue to hold true to those traits. Even if they occasionally let you down, you probably know the person well enough to understand that his or her intentions were good. Isn't that what matters?

Trusting is also about mindfulness because it has to do with noticing. You *notice* if someone reaches out to check on your well-being. You notice if someone continually flakes out on dinner plans. You notice which friends help you out in a pinch. You certainly notice when your spouse drives you somewhere—and you arrive in one piece. Once you've noticed someone's integrity, you can give that person the gift of your trust. They're earned it.

And it *is* a gift. When you trust someone fully and completely, giving up the illusion of control, you're also allowing the other person to show up for you and take care of you. That feels wonderful for the other person. When the time comes for you to take the wheel, you just might be surprised at the gift of trust you get in return.

Week 39

Do I Really Need Another Pair Of Shoes?

Years ago, I was introduced to the concept of STINGs (short-term immediate-need gratification). I love that acronym because it's easy to remember and most of us have had the experience of wanting something now, now, now. It sometimes seems that we've come to expect an immediate response to any and all of our urges. How mindful is it to live a life where we're always quick to satisfy every desire?

Actually, immediate gratification is the opposite of mindfulness. Impulsivity is not conducive to making informed or thoughtful decisions, noticing what you need, slowing down enough to examine your sudden urges, or deliberately doing nothing at all. Some of us resort to impulsivity when we need distraction from uncomfortable feelings like boredom, worry, or anger, and we treat ourselves to an online shopping spree or a few shots of tequila. How about constantly checking voice mail or text messages? These STINGs interfere with a variety of other responses that can help you build patience, gain insight, or develop more satisfying relationships. In other words, every itch does not need to be scratched—at least not immediately.

I don't want to minimize how deeply you may crave that distraction at times, but it's important to recognize that our culture—with immediate access to almost anything—makes it difficult to practice patience, whether you are waiting for a video to download or a friend to finish a sentence. As a parent, I have used some methods of distraction with my son. When he was younger, I'd try to redirect his attention if I noticed that he was uneasy or ready to have a meltdown. I'd shove something in his hand or bounce some toy in front of his face so he wouldn't cry. As he got older, I would try to soothe him by distracting him from some slight at school or with friends. Then, as my mindfulness practice took hold, I began to help him build tolerance by talking things out and asking him questions about his uncomfortable feelings so that he wouldn't have the immediate need to distract himself from them. Just addressing these emotions directly has helped him recognize that most feelings aren't born from crisis and can be tolerated.

How do we learn to tolerate our feelings, especially when they're uncomfortable? Not too long ago, I'd walk it off in the mall after a fight with my husband. That often became my go-to distraction when I didn't want to deal with my feelings of anger and disappointment. I'd wander in and out of the stores while ruminating about how right I was and how my feelings were hurt. What's different now, with more mindful awareness, is that I'm able to take a breath and delay my overzealous reaction to my feelings. I can be calm and reply accordingly (without screaming, yelling, or shopping it off).

When my son is angry about something, he used to run upstairs and stick his headphones on to distract himself from me and to avoid further discussion about what he did wrong (or endure more yelling). Now, he is able to stand in the room, cross-armed, and simply tell me that I'm overreacting (in a surprisingly calm way!) Sometimes, I am. I'm grateful when he chooses to withstand the storm long enough to grab my attention and when he chooses to express his feelings. I'm quite impressed by his unwavering stance when he defends himself, in the moment, rather than avoiding the primal urge to flee.

The trick, for my son or anyone, is to catch yourself during the onslaught of aversive feelings. Notice your body and mind's urge to distance yourself from the uncomfortable situation with another game of Candy Crush or by browsing a discount-shopping site. Wait it out. Count to five and attempt to gently shift your mind and behavior, perhaps by changing your environment. Notice your resistance, stubbornness, and eagerness to give in to your autopilot behavior. If you can cope with the discomfort for five seconds, noticing and breathing, you may realize that your urge, whatever it is, is really masking feelings of anxiety or fear.

Maybe you are procrastinating on a project or delaying a phone call that needs to be made. Maybe you're bored or a bit depressed, and it feels easier to browse Facebook than to sit quietly. If you're lonely, do you reach for the sleeve of cookies or bag of chips? Tolerating your feelings for even a short time with the help of your own self-soothing voice takes practice, but the more you make a point of waiting out that discomfort, the easier it will be to.let your need for instant gratification or distraction pass. By delaying your response, you're teaching yourself patience and honing your ability to distinguish an actual crisis from a passing desire.

Patience may be a virtue, but it is also a skill. To truly experience it, you must practice it again and again and find the reward in waiting. It may show up in your wallet when you delay that desire to cyber shop or on the scale when you walk on by the chocolate chip cookies in the pantry. Anyway you look at it, if you take five seconds to notice the urge for immediate gratification and let yourself breathe, it's sure to pass.

Week 40

Be-ing in a Marriage

When I was twenty-three, I married a man I met in college. Though I was only nineteen when we got together, I was sure that we were soul mates. We both had a sense of adventure and optimism, similar family values, and liked the same music. We weren't that gushy kind of PDA couple, but we had cute nicknames for each other and were truly in love. We were young, and the decision to marry felt as if we were taking a leap into adulthood together. I was happy. I'd done the college thing (check). Next on my list was getting hitched.

I assumed that we would grow old together and that my fairy-tale life was already underway. I had no reason to doubt that my happiness would continue. And it did—for a while.

Then, stuff happened, as it always does. We moved from the city to the suburbs (for my ex's job), and I grew restless. I began to hate my own job—and the next few to follow. We started trying for a baby, but I couldn't get pregnant. My husband dealt with his disappointments in his way, and I dealt in mine. I became resentful, sometimes brooding, but mostly angry and judgmental. We stopped communicating. We spent less and less time together and vented to our respective friends.

It felt as though my commitment to being married stopped being a priority. We forgot our purpose as a couple: to live a life of adventure and love. Instead, each of us pursued our individual needs to be happier, which led us to going our separate ways. If we were at all mindful—and if I had the ability to understand the term back then—our intention was not on marriage and commitment. It was on pleasing ourselves, individually, with little left over for compassion, support, or empathy for the other's hopes and dreams.

Ultimately, in pursuit of those hopes and dreams, I left my marriage. I hoped that eventually I would find another partner who would give me what I hadn't found the first time around: a life of adventure and love.

Over time—and with insight gained from wise friends, therapist, and other forms of soul-searching—I took responsibility for my failed marriage. As months and then years passed, I grew determined to learn from my mistakes and find a relationship that was built on mutual support of each other's goals and aspirations. The next time around, I was determined that my future husband and I would ride out any and all of life's inevitable bumps and painful periods together.

A few years into my Los Angeles life, I met him. I was thirty-two years old and had been dating in my new hometown, but I hadn't met anyone quite like him. He was my Renaissance man: creative, well-read, a lover of art and travel, a man who could play chess, fix toilets and cars, and build stuff. He had a good job, he had interests, he had close friends, and he loved me. He, too, was divorced and wanted to find a mate who would support and inspire him through life's beautiful and sometimes-treacherous journey. We were both willing and hopeful that this second chance at love would last.

Partly because of our failed first marriages, we made this commitment to each other consciously—with deliberate intention—something we hadn't done with our previous spouses, only assuming that we could traverse anything that came our way. We vowed that being married would be our priority, come what may, and that we would work through any and all difficult tribulations.

Within a short time, of course, life's challenges began to test us. We were faced with the illness of loved ones. I started graduate school, was working full-time, and was trying to get pregnant. My husband changed his job and experienced some frustrations in the transition. We were living in a small apartment and had accumulated some debt. It took an enormous amount of dedication, determination, and commitment to face all of these challenges, but we did face them—together. We chose to use our savings to pay off our debts and start from scratch. With my husband's support, I quit my job and focused on school. We were also committed to spending as much time together and having as much fun together as we could, which would remind us of the love we felt. The notion that things would get too difficult or that we would quit at this early stage of our newly cemented relationship was not even close to a possibility. These were all challenges that we could overcome by making tough choices, mindfully, together.

It's impossible to plan for all the curves that life can throw your way and avoid any down periods in a marriage. We had our share of good fortune when we eventually had a son, bought our first home, and even had some extra savings to do the traveling we loved. When the economy took a turn for the worse and my mother-in-law succumbed to cancer, our emotions sometimes got the better of us. There were times we pulled away from one another. My husband would become silent and stoic, and I would be angry and judgmental. I had *seen* it in my first marriage, but now I *noticed*. I saw the destruction our behaviors and emotions could bring and decided to put a stop to it.

I reminded my husband of our commitment to sticking out our marriage—come what may. Divorce was not an option. In a quiet moment, we talked about our commitment and our willingness to remain together. We sought counseling with a gifted psychologist who kindly and gently coaxed us back to a steadfast resolve, and we began to heal together. We were reminded of our differences, but our intention to stay wholeheartedly connected to one another was more important.

Being mindful in a marriage means being aware of yourself and how you bring kindness, love, appreciation, acceptance, respect, and dedication to your union. It requires an intention to stay together through the ups and downs, then returning to that intention, over and over, knowing that even when things are tough, you're in it together.

Week 41

&

How to Have Fun at Your Own Party

I love to cook and entertain, and if the evening includes a round or two of Pictionary, all the better. For me, having guests over to my home—for a backyard barbecue, game night, or my BFF's birthday—is an opportunity to shower the people I love with gratitude, appreciation, and joy. That's my intention, anyway. As much as I love to throw a good party, until recently, I found much of the process incredibly stressful. Overwhelmed by the details of planning and prepping, my mood would often get the best of me. I'd growl, talk to myself, bark directives to my helpers (aka my husband and son), and generally lose patience. Burdened by expectation and anxiety, I would rush around cooking, cleaning, and prepping and then not feel like a part of the celebration. I felt like a servant, flitting around, cleaning up, and refilling empty glasses. I was there—but not actually *there*. I'd forgotten my intention.

Thankfully, during one of those stressful moments (while shouting at my husband to move a table and freaking out because we'd run out of cute cocktail napkins), I had a realization. *If there was ever a time to be present, this is it.* Forget the cocktail napkins. I needed to pause, take notice, and shift my mood to match my intention, which, on that afternoon, was showing my BFF my love and appreciation by hosting her milestone birthday celebration.

After I took a breath, I reminded myself to focus on the details and notice the decorations, the food, the cute outfit I'd chosen. When I remember to attend to all of the details step-by-step, with calm precision and intention, my anxiety soon lifts.

Just as important, I remind myself to add some fun to the process. I turn up the music, open the windows, or light some candles to get into the right state of mind. I do this deliberately, so that I can stay focused on doing what I need to do. That way, when my guests arrive, I'm fully present—and we get to enjoy the party together.

Week 42

Taco Tuesday 2.0

From time to time, I come home with no energy—or inspiration—to make dinner. Worse, I feel absolutely bored with every part of my daily routine. I wish I could just phone everything in, especially the food. Cue the mom guilt.

I've learned that, without too much planning, it's possible to break out of those predictable habits (dinner in front of the TV again?) and transform regular, boring mealtimes into something that offers an element of surprise and some family bonding.

Take Taco Tuesday. I love this meal because it's so easy to prepare, especially once I've stocked my freezer and pantry with the requisite ground meat, spices, and tortillas. I've prepared this so often that I can fix the tacos while standing on my head with a glass of sangria in my hand. There's something to be said about routine, however predictable, especially after a long day's work.

Still, even Taco Tuesday can get a bit monotonous. The good news is that you don't always need to make a big dramatic change in your daily life—or your dinner—to better notice and appreciate each moment. To mix things up, I deliberately make Taco Tuesday an *occasion*. I'll find the Mexican blanket I bought while on vacation and use it as a tablecloth, grab my "good" red napkins, and add a sprinkle of Latin music to the scene. This may seem silly or juvenile, but how much effort and time does it take to make this familiar dinner feel new again?

At the least, I get a few smiles from my son and husband. I think of it as Taco Tuesday 2.0.

What's *your* go-to meal? Is it meatless Monday? Fishy Friday? Take a minute to think of an improvisation that might nudge you out of your comfort zone, excite you, and get you into that fresh beginner's mind so you can experience the meal as if for the first time.

Week 43

Be True to You

It took years for me to realize that I'm like a tortoise. I'm the kind of person who sticks to an endeavor until all the i's are dotted and t's are crossed. I meander down the long, deliberate path that leads me to what I truly want (like taking ten years to get licensed as a therapist!). I didn't always recognize or appreciate this trait, but once I've made a commitment, I hang in and do the work—no matter long it takes. It took a long time to know myself in this way and not rely too much on the opinions of others. Mindfulness helped me get there.

Sometimes, I stick with things for too long. I've remained in relationships past their expiration date, gotten stuck in jobs that were not fulfilling, and, after four painful rounds of IVF, realized that I was done with that (and was lucky enough to get pregnant once I was through!) Once the light clicks on, my instinct kicks in. I said good-bye to a career that no longer served me. I've ended one-sided friendships. I decided that it was better to appreciate our one child than to expend any more effort—and endure any more disappointment—while trying to grow my family. All of these journeys, however long they take, begin with a commitment to the road ahead. In my case, it was the *long, long* road ahead. To endure that long road, I've needed to practice self-awareness and self-acceptance. This is who I am. Slow and steady is the way I roll, and that's okay.

I don't always love that things take me a while, but when I deviate from my routine and try to speed up the process, I trip myself up. I make mistakes or ignore my inner voice that tells me to slow down and take it easy. Sometimes, when I'm in a whirlwind of activity, my bestie will chuckle, knowing that I'm not truly in my groove. She knows I'm taking a haphazard and disorganized approach to completing my task, however busy and efficient I may look. Ultimately, it ends badly. This has been true whether I'm rushing to chop vegetables for salad with a large knife or trying to make a major life decision (like accepting a crappy job for the salary or dating a guy I sensed was just wrong for me). I've learned over time that going slow and being deliberate is the best way for me.

Embracing my inner tortoise has also helped me let go of judgment and expectations and focus on the life I am living. I take one day at a time, moving purposely, slowly, and intentionally toward a particular destination with less anxiety and more gratitude, especially when I'm finally done! I've come to have faith in myself because my method has led to a track record of positive outcomes, if not speedy ones.

I'm not saying that being a tortoise is better than being a hare. I marveled at my peers who finished their degrees and got licensed in record time. I am amazed at neighbors who get their Christmas lights up the day after Thanksgiving and friends who send out thank-you cards immediately after their wedding.

Mindfulness has helped me develop the ability to know what works for me and what doesn't. Slowness works. Speediness? Not so much. I urge you to know and honor who *you* are and to move through life at a pace that is comfortable for you. The journey is what matters.

Week 44

Travel Porn and Other Guilty Pleasures

I'm going to say something that might surprise you: Browsing the web or using Instagram or Snapchat can become experiences to savor so that you don't end up feeling as if two hours of your life have just disappeared down a black hole. The secret is mindfulness.

I love scouring the Internet to get ideas for my next vacation or next meal (aka browsing travel and food porn). But when I do this mindlessly, scrolling through my favorite sites without much intention or the desire to learn anything new, I realize that I've shifted into procrastinating or avoidance.

When I scan my favorite sites mindfully, I try to give the task my complete attention—just as I do with anything that sparks my interest and curiosity. I engage fully, starting by setting an intention to fire up my imagination and get inspired. Food and travel do those things for me. Finding new recipes and planning my next trip make me happy—even if I never actually get to those destinations or make that fabulous meal. Isn't dreaming the point of taking a time-out on the Internet in the first place?

The same goes for reading a trashy novel, watching *The Bachelor,* or perusing a tabloid magazine. Many women feel guilty about doing these things. If you're doing them with your full attention and enjoying the chance to spend time with yourself, then you are living and behaving mindfully. How to tell? If you're surfing the web or doing anything just to pass the time, as we all occasionally do, you'll end up feeling empty, unproductive, guilty, and maybe even a bit irritable.

Are you avoiding work or relying on the Internet (or whatever your particular vice of choice) to detach emotionally? Take a moment to check in with your intention. Do you have one? If not, set one. Your free time is limited; why not make the most of it? That doesn't mean everything you do must be productive or educational, but it does need purpose. This purpose alone can be your intention, and it can be as simple as cheering yourself up. Listening to music, surfing the web, and even watching silly cat videos can lift your spirits and relax you.

When you set your intention and deliberately give yourself the gift (and permission) of spending time that isn't explicitly productive or informative, you'll *feel* the results rather than feeling guilty.

Week 45

The Perfect Parent and Other Annoying Myths

The biggest challenge of my life is raising my son. Yes, I've had to overcome lots of difficult hurdles, including dealing with my own health issues, my aging parents, a busy and sometimes distracted husband, and some relationship disappointments. But by far, the most difficult thing I have had to do is to be a parent to a little boy.

As a female, I sometimes feel ill-equipped to handle my son's sometimes boy-centric quirks. He loves fart humor and hates showering. He's obsessed with TV and YouTube, and he has a tendency to be disorganized. There are little frustrations too like when he leaves the lights on no matter how often I remind him to turn them off, forgets to brush his teeth before going to school, or leaves a heap of dirty clothes next to the hamper. Those are just some of the things that leave me infuriated. Perhaps, if you're a parent, you can relate?

Just the other day, I found myself losing my cool when I learned that my son had failed to turn in yet another homework assignment. He'd done the work; he simply didn't give it to the teacher. At that moment, my autopilot reaction got the best of me. I started screaming about deadlines and their importance for getting into college (he's in middle school). I was barely looking at the poor guy, but I scared the living bejeezus out of him. It was quite ridiculous, and I felt awful about it.

I'm a therapist—and I lost it! I'm supposed to have ways of dealing with these things. After all, I help clients cope with similar situations every week. I suggest that they make homework charts for their kids, give positive feedback, or try a reward system. I've used these interventions myself. Sometimes, they even work, but only when I am being mindful, compassionate, and patient.

In the middle of my meltdown, I noticed my body changing: my temperature was rising, my heart was racing, and my throat was burning (from yelling). Those were all signals I needed to realize that I had to calm down. I did, and I apologized for losing it. Without my mindful meditation practice, I might have continued to scream, leaving both of us in tears. I may not have felt responsible for my own crazed reaction and blamed my twelve-year-old. I'm not a perfect mother, far from it, but mindfulness has helped me notice that there are other options besides negativity. In this case, I was able to choose another option, take a breath, and compose myself.

It's easy to forget that kids are learning all the time. They are learning to relate to others, organize their stuff, share, complete tasks, and be responsible for turning in their homework. We must be patient with their learning, and it takes intention to be patient. By practicing patience, we provide a model for our children to learn patience themselves. If not from us, from whom?

There's a saying in meditation: "You should sit for twenty minutes a day—unless you're too busy. Then you should sit for an hour." The same goes for patience. It takes dedication and practice to grow this trait, but it can start with something as simple as paying attention to your breathing and then tuning into your heart rate, your temper, and your attitude when you are with your child or your mate. Try noticing these signals when things are good too. Make a point of sharing your knowledge. ("I feel really happy with you right now. You remembered to turn in your project on time!") Once you recognize your calm state, you can use it as an anchor when things are not quite so serene and shift an immediate, negative reaction to one that's more conscious and kinder.

Week 46

❦

Just Say Yes!

A few years ago, I watched a movie called *Yes Man*. Jim Carrey's character had to say *yes* to any question asked of him. I know I'm not the first person to be affected by this movie, but I had my own Jim Carrey moment when I was standing in line with my husband in downtown Los Angeles, waiting to get into a Train concert.

As I was waiting, a woman behind me was telling her friends about other wonderful performances she'd seen at this theater, located inside the Grammy Museum, a special two hundred-seat space that showcases musicians and performers of all levels.

I couldn't help but insert myself into the animated conversation, and soon we were all chatting about Maroon 5, another one of my favorite bands.

One of the women, Monika, asked, "Hey, any of you ladies want to join me in New York City next Tuesday to catch a Maroon 5 performance? I have an extra ticket. Oh, and I work at an airline and can get you a friend rate if you'd like to join me." *Really? This is my chance to say yes!*

I glanced at my husband, and he gave me the thumbs-up. I jumped right in! If I could figure out a way to manage my carpool commitments and dinners, I'd be able to get there, despite the fact that it was only three days away. I was calculating how to drop my son off at school, arrange to have someone pick him up and watch him for the afternoon, take an early flight, see the concert, crash at my friend's place, and catch the next morning's flight back to Los Angeles. Done! The concert was amazing.

The whole thing was spontaneous, right? But without deliberate intention and, the support of my amazing husband, that experience never would have happened. I may have stood next to Monika and smiled and *wished* I could join her, but with that Jim Carrey movie in mind, on some level, I was deliberately searching for an opportunity to take action and say *yes* to whatever came my way. It could have been any number of opportunities—a new job or a new friend. I made the choice to be mindful of the opportunity and then acted on it. That was my intention.

Opportunities that seemingly fall from the sky—where you find yourself lucky—don't actually happen out of the blue. They require intention. The desire and conscious effort to stay open to all possibilities is what creates these magical moments—whether you're searching for love and come upon someone who might be the one or are taking a stroll on a trip and find yourself in the middle of a street party. Being ready for these moments makes for a richer, more adventurous life.

Monika remains my friend. We've since made it to the Grammy Awards (after applying to be seat-fillers online) as well as other concerts and performances. She loves live shows too, and I am so grateful for her willingness and enthusiasm to embrace anything that's thrown her path.

There are more opportunities to say *yes* than you might think. You don't have to eavesdrop, like I did, to find them. With intention, by taking notice, you can act when the opportunity arises and seize the moment. If it's what you want, whatever it is, say *yes!*

Week 47

＆

LOL more often

Recently, I attended a Laughing Yoga workshop at my local chapter of the California Association for Marriage and Family Therapists. The woman who led the group had an actual certification to conduct such classes and was trained in the art of practicing laughter. To be clear, I'm talking about laughter for the sake of laughing—without humor, jokes, or sketch comedy. I was interested because I am a laugher. I basically laugh when I'm nervous, when I make dumb mistake, and when my BFF cracks me up (which, lucky for me, is quite often.)

We all filled out a questionnaire to measure our levels of enthusiasm, energy, mood, optimism, and stress. We settled into this Laughing Yoga workshop, a group of thirty or so therapists in our seats. I felt uncertain, and I noticed that others seemed to feel awkward as well. I had heard about classes where everyone was supposed to force a laugh as a group. I'm all for laughing and enjoying myself, but even so, I was skeptical.

The instructor had us gather in a large circle. She told us that we were going to learn a new type of yoga exercise, a new type of breathing. "You are all going to experience changes in your disposition, attitude, and heart rate." She made me feel more comfortable with this idea, and I was willing. Why not do something that sounded quirky and silly amidst the safety and comfort of other therapists and peers?

We began with some basic exercises to get us in the mood. We clapped and shouted, "Ho, ho, yay, yay, yay!" That brought out chuckles across the room. We practiced laughing out loud, which immediately made everyone smile. It was very silly, but being deliberate about this exercise actually brought up some strong feelings in the room. Some were reminded of their childhood friends laughing and playing, and others were reminded that there was not enough laughter in their own homes. As we continued to laugh out loud, following specific instructions to prompt our laugher, I found that I was laughing on cue, and I couldn't stop smiling. The people around me were smiling too.

After the laughing exercises were complete, we were asked to answer the same questions we'd answered at the beginning of the hour. Initially, most of my measurements were average (five out of ten). Afterward, they were about 20 percent better, meaning that my happiness or contentment had increased significantly.

Laughing and smiling has an immediate affect on mood and attitude. It can shift your perspective toward the positive. Scientifically speaking, there are many studies that suggest smiling boosts immunity, releases feel-good endorphins, and makes other people feel good too. All it takes is moving the muscles in your mouth in an upward motion.

Certainly, when you're arguing with someone, smiling (even if you don't feel like it) or using humor can lighten up the situation. What's surprising is that a forced laugh or smile can also make a difference, according to research. Oddly, your brain can't tell the difference between a fake smile or laugh and a real one—the endorphins start flowing just the same. So why not mindfully and deliberately try this with your girlfriend, partner, or child? You may giggle at the absurdity of it, but you'll be laughing either way.

Week 48

Stop the Body Wars

I've always hated my thighs. I've never been one of those waiflike girls. My frame is solid, falling smack within the average range. As I got older, I developed a curvy shape, which made it hard to find a pair of jeans that fit. As my BFF can attest, I have tried every diet (grapefruit, no carbs/all carbs, smoothies, cayenne pepper detox) and exercise regimen (Tae Bo, kickboxing, CrossFit, spinning, Barre) to feel good enough to quiet that inner voice that insists my body is not okay.

Maybe, when it comes to your body, you've also gone after the quick fix, and then felt disappointment when the results didn't materialize. The solution, I've discovered, is not to try another diet or even Tae Bo. The solution is to practice patience, loving-kindness, and non-judgment with whatever shape your body happens to be in right now.

When my nasty-body thoughts appeared, I began do what has helped me in other situations where I seem to be stuck. I paid attention to that mean voice, but I did not heed its advice (to think less of myself or cover up my body with baggy clothes.) I noticed the self-criticism, and I deliberately chose not to let it affect me. What began to happen is the evil voice got softer. It stopped screeching at me when I looked in the mirror as I got dressed each morning. How exactly did it happen? Like any other issue that seemingly controls us, it takes a lot of self-compassion and acceptance to move beyond body-shaming and live a life that's (relatively) free of judgment. Mindfulness can have a major impact on your body image because it is a continuous exercise in this kind of non-judgment and loving-kindness.

Truly being grateful for my ability to do yoga, walk a few miles and feel the air in my lungs, and laugh out loud helps quiet that ugly voice. I make a point of saying how grateful I am. I write it in my journal. I deliberately practice gratitude—again and again, every day.

The next time and the next time and the next time you hear an inner voice suggesting that any part of your body is ugly, fat, or out of proportion, find one thing that works and looks or feels okay and give it your full attention. Your left knee? That's fine—focus on it. Spend a moment, every day, noticing this body part and feeling grateful for it. You will find, with time, that your malevolent voice fades, becoming less incessant. Getting to that place of inner stillness requires deliberate and continuous attention; after all, you've amped up that mean-girl voice your entire life.

Practicing gratitude, loving-kindness, and non-judgment isn't always easy, particularly toward ourselves. Most of us haven't learned these skills. Some of us may even find them uncomfortable or self-indulgent. As odd as it may seem, by practicing gratitude for your body (its strength, its ability to get up and take you through your day, its capacity to love and protect others) you'll begin to appreciate the kinder voice within you—and maybe feel compassion for that negative voice as you finally let it go and embrace what you've got.

Week 49

=== 🦋 ===

Didn't Get What You Want? Get Over It a Little Easier

It's inevitable that you will experience disappointment in your life and times when things don't go your way. Being disappointed is a crappy feeling. We've all endured it: being bummed that your kid didn't make As (or Bs), being hurt when friends leave you out, being angry when your spouse has to work late, being disappointed in yourself for not following through on a commitment.

The way you handle these let downs determines your ability to reduce your suffering. If you allow the feeling to linger too long, ruminating in dejection, you can sink further into the hole, miring yourself in negative emotions like fear, resentment, or even self-loathing.

Mindfulness, on the other hand, can help you notice and regulate this tendency to get depressed or wallow. By *noticing* your bad feelings, you can stop yourself from falling into an abyss that robs you of future opportunities and happiness. You can ruminate mindlessly, wondering when someone will come along and take the pain away—or you can mindfully observe what you're feeling in the moment without judging.

You can choose to process your feelings. *Process* is a therapy term for *talking it out* or expressing your full emotions while observing yourself. It is not the same thing as ruminating, complaining, or wishing it wasn't so. Instead, processing can help you hash out your feelings with someone you trust in a contained way so that you can stay present despite the disappointment. This makes it easier to get on with the rest of your day instead of becoming consumed with disconsolate thoughts. Knowing the difference between talking about your feelings and wallowing in self-pity is the key to moving from anger to acceptance.

When my son started middle school, it was a bumpy transition full of missed assignments and failed pop quizzes. *Oh, joy.* My ability to talk about my feelings to my son, my husband, my friends, and my therapist has kept me steadfast and compassionate, and it has made me a better parent. My BFF points out when I'm being too critical or judgmental so that I can be more aware when I'm talking so my emotions don't overwhelm me or create distance between us. It also helps to purposefully remind myself that any one incident—a failed quiz, a missed homework assignment—does not mean that all future tests or assignments will go the same way.

When I choose this deliberate approach to dealing with disappointment instead of mindlessly brooding, I am able to stick to my intention of helping myself through disappointment instead of letting my feelings run away with me.

Week 50

Get Your Sexy On

In the first *Sex and the City* movie, there's a scene where Miranda is having sex with her husband and blurts out, "Let's get this over with already!" Steve responds, "We never have sex, and you already want this to be over?"

Both statements made an impression on me.

Many of us can agree that we like sex. Maybe we even want more sex. But when it comes to deliberately making the time and the effort for sex to actually happen, most women I know (including me) rarely create the opportunity. We use all the usual excuses (too tired, no time) to delay and avoid, and we end up feeling more distanced from our partners.

Why do we do this when the coming together of two people can be a reminder of just how good sex can feel? After all, if you're looking for an opportunity to be happier in your relationship, it seems like a no-brainer that if you had the chance to have sex, you'd take it. But in real life, sex doesn't work that way—at least not for women. Before I can let myself go in the bedroom, I want to feel paid attention to and be noticed. Sex, for me, starts in the morning with a smile, a phone call to check in, and my husband taking out the trash (without me having to ask).

Feeling more connected begins with an intention to create more intimacy—and a conscious desire to make sex a priority despite the usual excuses. If you're waiting for your mate to make the first move, then you're missing the point. You can and *should* make the first move.

Be deliberate. Create the intimacy. Being kind and loving and telling your partner how much you appreciate him (or her) is a good start. Men are pretty simple in some ways. Most simply want sex. They're happy to get it when they can. In some cases, they even marry because they think sex will be a sure thing. But being deliberate and mindfully creating intimacy has to do with more than sex. It starts with your attitude and how you show up in your relationship. Show your appreciation. Express it. The key to a man's heart is letting him know that he is appreciated. I make sure my husband knows how much I appreciate the way he works hard to keep our family safe and secure. My words help him feel more connected to me. Sex also makes him feel this way.

If you're waiting for something magical to happen to bring you closer to your partner, stop waiting. Instead, set your intention to be more intimate. Deliberately and purposefully make time for sex in the morning before work or on a Saturday afternoon. Bring the best you to the bedroom—the loving, kind, and attentive you. If you're so inspired, break out the sexy bra and panties you've been hiding in the back of your drawer. Shave your legs! Just as important is bringing what might be missing from your day-to-day life: intimacy in the form of affection, attention, quietness together, tenderness, and acceptance. When you're aware of your attitude and are willing to let your guard down and show your love, you can create more connection. Your partner will be happier for it and will show you love (and intimacy) in return.

Week 51

On Your Mark, Get Set, Sit Pretty!

Are you ready to try this? Being here, being still, and reading this book is a perfect place to move from informal meditation and everyday mindfulness to trying a formal sitting mediation.

You don't have to go to a weekly class. You can download an app and meditate at home. One of my favorites, Relaxed Melodies, includes guided meditations to help with focus, confidence, creativity, and procrastination. I also like Take a Break, a wonderful app designed to help you squeeze in a quick meditation wherever you happen to be.

You can make it even easier. Get comfortable, close your eyes, notice your mind (busy or calm), observe your breathing, and set an intention to return to your breath as often as possible (which may be every few seconds). When your mind starts to drift, gently return your focus to your breathing. Notice the physical feeling of your inhalations and exhalations, the air going in and out of your nostrils. Notice your belly rising and falling. Continue bringing your attention back to your breathing. Know that your mind is going to wander, and when it does, nudge it back to your intention and notice your breathing again.

That's it! That's a formal sitting meditation (and you don't even have to sit!). Start with two minutes (you can set a timer) and notice your mind, but don't engage in any of your thoughts. Simply notice that the thoughts happen to be there and continue on your way as if clouds are your thoughts. They'll appear and disappear at whim. You can gradually try sitting for longer periods, using sound or your other senses as an anchor.

My favorite way to meditate is outside in my garden or on the beach. The heat of the sun and the breeze in my hair are my anchor points. My mind still drifts, but with intention, I bring it back, again and again, to linger on the feeling of the sun on my face. Bliss.

Week 52

Welcome Home

When I walked into my first meditation retreat in 2010, I noticed a blackboard scrawled with the words "Welcome Home." I was a novice back then, and I wasn't sure of the meaning. I think I may have rolled my eyes and uttered a silent scream at this "Zen-ny" phrase. It sounded suspiciously woo-woo to me.

As I've come to learn, "welcome home" isn't woo-woo, and it doesn't have anything to do with a house or an apartment. The phrase refers to an awakening, to gaining deeper insight, and understanding who you are and where you've come from. As a therapist, I can tell you that mindful meditation is not the only way to achieve this kind of self-knowledge, but it has certainly paved my way.

Besides tipping me off that I'm a tortoise—slow and deliberate on my life path—my meditation practice has helped me look at myself and know myself more intimately, kindly, and gently, with less judgment. I have come to feel more content with who I am—flaws and all. This understanding and self-knowledge has led me to a place of feeling at home with myself. I am more comfortable, more at ease.

How do you achieve this feeling—other than snuggling up in your living room with the fireplace blazing? It starts with using all of your senses to increase your awareness of what's around you—the aromas, sounds, sights, and flavors. This isn't just an exercise. The more you become aware of what's around you in your everyday life, the more you'll notice the little stuff while you tend to your family, your job, your fitness, and your commute. You'll feel a greater capacity to keep using your senses more fully and keep noticing things. You'll also get better at noticing when you're *not* noticing.

What does this have to do with feeling at home with who you are? How can simply noticing things bring inner knowledge? What's the big deal? The key is to go *beyond* noticing the exterior and recognize what truly resonates with you on a deeper level—how you *feel* about the things you notice when you become aware of them. Think of these as the tiny pauses during dinner with your family or a walk in the park with your dog. They're essentially the intimacy and connection you feel when you recognize the gravity of a single moment. At these times, you can reflect on who you really are—and more truly be yourself—because you are fully present, listening and paying attention.

Remember that cup of coffee in the morning that you smelled and anticipated until you took your first sip? Did it bring delight or relief once the caffeine was coursing through your system? The greater your ability to sustain attention to these ordinary things and listen deeply to others, the richer your life will be. This kind of awareness has a way of revealing what you need to spend time on or not.

Once you've broken free from life's pile of insignificant activities and obligations, lifted your head (from your smartphone), and noticed, you can know yourself better. The better you know yourself, including what motivates you, what you fear, and what you appreciate, the easier it is to accept your uniqueness and your quirks. You'll also feel more confident when you arrive at major life crossroads or face ordinary decisions.

Following the path of insight is not always easy. When I'm creating something, whether a meal or a drawing, I feel joyful and free. I'm also aware of a little voice inside me, whispering that what I'm doing is not quite good enough or that I'm not being productive. I may never be able to get that voice to shut up completely. What *has* changed, because of the insight I've gained through my mindfulness practice, is that I can give a nod to those feelings and thoughts. I can observe them and continue to do what I love to do. That's liberating.

Knowing yourself and sticking with your conviction, despite those inner negative whispers, takes courage. If you've gotten to this point in the book, I'm guessing that it's the path you're choosing. You ultimately hope to live your life with full participation, knowledge, authenticity, and contentment. Happiness is great. We all want it. But happiness, like all feelings, is transitory. Isn't it nice to know that you can feel at home with yourself—comfortable and at ease—whenever and wherever you choose?

Last Thoughts

Your *Sitting Pretty* Tool Kit

There are many books on mindfulness and meditation, but these particular books have had a profound affect on me, especially in helping me, reminding me, and enlightening me to become the person I am right now.

Books

Jon Kabat-Zinn, *Wherever You Go, There You Are* (Hachette Books: January 2005). To help gain a deeper knowledge and understanding of mindfulness and its everyday practical use, I love the references he uses as a parent and how we all have similar human struggles.

Jon Kabat-Zinn, *Full Catastrophe Living* (Bantom, September 2013). A more in-depth lesson on formal mindful meditation, using Mindfulness-Based Stress-Reduction techniques developed by Kabat-Zinn. While my brother was recovering from knee surgery, he told me about this book. I soon picked it up and learned more about reducing stress and pain through meditation.

Geneen Roth, *Women, Food, and God* (Scribner, February 2011). A spiritual approach and look at how we view food. It turns out that our relationship with food is a reflection of how we feel about *almost* everything.

Thich Nhat Hahn, *True Love: A practice for Awakening the Heart* (Shambhala, October 2011). A little book that really inspires, filled with short chapters intended to help cultivate more love and cherish and respect the impact you have on your loved ones. I must have referenced this book with every couple I've helped in my therapy practice and gifted it to my friends and my husband. It reminds me what love really is, which is why it sits on my nightstand.

Viktor E. Frankl, *Man's Search for Meaning* (Beacon Press, June 2006). A psychiatrist and survivor of the Nazi death camps, the author questions suffering and helps us understand that it must have a purpose. This book puts life into perspective.

Apps for Guided Meditations

Calm—Soothing sounds and gently guided meditations for seven days of focus, calm, sleep, happiness, gratitude, and self-esteem. There are also timed unguided meditations.

White Noise—Forty great sounds to help you relax during the day and sleep at night.

Stop, Breathe, and Think—Guided meditations designed and tailored to your mood. I recommend this app for beginners.

Headspace—A popular, simple, and easy-to-use guided meditation app.

Blogs and Websites

Mrs. Mindfulness—Meli O'Brien is a mindfulness teacher and practitioner who offers solid advice and helpful tools to master mindfulness for novices and experts alike.

www.Mindful.org—A great resource filled with tidbits of information that educate and inspire readers to become more mindful. It is also a magazine.

www.centerhealthyminds.org—Center for Healthy Minds: University of Wisconsin, Madison—There are countless universities studying mindfulness, but this site offers particularly intriguing (and easy-to-read) studies on how mindfulness affects the brain.

The World Happiness Report—An interesting study is done every year, analyzing happiness around the world. In the latest ranking, the 2017 report ranks Norway #1 and the United States #14.

Acknowledgments

I want to thank a whole bunch of people who inspired me, taught me, and cheered me on through this process. First, Kelly Sullivan-Walden, who read my travel journal I kept on the life-changing yoga retreat in France, the year I turned fifty, and encouraged me to keep writing to inspire others to live a more mindful life. Her enthusiasm and support is what prompted me to write this book.

A special thank you to Paula Derrow, editor extraordinaire, who also assured me that I could write and that I had something important to share.

A warm and loving thank you to all of my special girlfriends who have always encouraged and supported my dreams. You really do know who you are!

Ian Goldey, my loving husband, who lived with me through the trials and tribulations (and a few meltdowns) of this project and was steadfast in his support.

Kathy Buratti, my BFF, who always brings humor and kindness to my sometimes critical self.

My meditation teacher and guru, Jerome Front, MFT, for whom I would not have had this journey (and continue to have) since 2010.

To my weekly meditation group friends—past and present: Kathy, Debbie, Julie, Jodi, Susan, Assaf, Steve, Christopher, and the countless others I've met in class and on retreats.

To my yoga teachers and community (Bikram Agoura Hills): Rachel, Erin, Ryan, Stephanie, Tom, Nancy, Holly, Brenda, Ayni, Steve, Joseph, Paula, Laurie E., Craig, and others who are in my heart. You've kept me sane.

To my brother and sister who always encourage and love me.

And, to my parents, who always—no matter what—tell me I should do it (whatever the *it* is!)